The grace of our Lord
overflowed for me
with the faith and love
that are in Christ Jesus.
1 Timothy 1:14

This book is a gift to

_____

from

_____

date

_____

Contents

Introduction

Now to Him who is able to do immeasurably more than all we ask or imagine, according to His power that is at work within us, to Him be glory. Ephesians 3:20–21, NIV

Immeasurably more.

Immeasurably more than all we ask.

Immeasurably more than all we imagine.

God is able to do immeasurably more . . . by His power at work within us. To Him be the glory!

(Did your jaw just drop too?) The One who created the universe and sent His Son to save you is the One who works within you. "For it is God who works in you, both to will and to work for His good pleasure" (Philippians 2:13).

The Lord works in infinite measure beyond all you ask in prayer . . . beyond your imagination. (Let that sink in.) He can do infinitely more than anything you can measure, and He chooses to work through you, His forgiven, chosen child in Christ.

Trust that God is mightily at work in you. In what ways does He provide immeasurably more? He gives you a limitless measure of His grace, love, power, purpose, peace, and more.

I can't wait for you to receive these affirmations of every good gift He gives to you in overflowing measure.

Imagine all that God can do . . . through you!

To Him be the glory,

Deb Burma

How to Use This Devotional Journal

I invite you to sit with your Savior. Curl up with your Bible and your favorite writing utensils. Lean in to learn, receive, and rest—alone or with a friend. *Immeasurably More* is a relational, conversational, richly scriptural devotional journal created for you . . . and it works in small group study settings too. Following every five or ten devotions, you can meet weekly or biweekly to review and discuss Scripture and the topics, along with your highlights and takeaways.

In addition to the daily devotional content and Bible passages, you will find a thought-provoking journal prompt,* followed by journaling or drawing space and a guided prayer. Notice that each prayer ends with ". . ." to encourage you to continue your conversation with the Lord, praying in Jesus' name.

*Allow the journal prompts to guide your personal devotion time, or choose to write or draw as the Spirit leads you, following your time in the Word.

IMMEASURABLY MORE
Grace

WHO GETS GRACE?

But God, being rich in mercy, because of the great love with which He loved us, even when we were dead in our trespasses, made us alive together with Christ—by grace you have been saved. Ephesians 2:4–5

What is grace and who gets it? What I understand as a grace period is when I have a few days between the statement date and when my account balance incurs additional charges. I get what it means to walk gracefully with good form and light feet. I know what to do when someone asks me to say grace before a meal. But do I "get" grace in the richest sense of the word? Do I understand divine grace, the grace of God, defined as undeserved, unearned favor? How can it be that He gives it to me freely, though I don't deserve it?

Sin did more than distance you and me from God. It severed us from Him completely. We were without hope, dead in our sin (Ephesians 2:1, 12). But God "made us alive together with Christ" (Ephesians 2:5), saving us by His grace through Christ's death and resurrection. Why would the Father choose to do such a thing? Because of His *great love* for us. While I struggle to wrap my mind around this great gift, I receive it by faith.

By His grace, time and again, Jesus has done immeasurably more through His forgiven followers than we could ask or imagine. As we take a glimpse into Scripture, we see His grace in action:

♥ *Grace* saved an adulterous woman from her captors . . . and from her sin (John 8:2–11). "Jesus stood up and said to her, 'Woman, where are they? Has no one condemned you?' She said, 'No one, Lord.' And

Jesus said, 'Neither do I condemn you; go, and from now on sin no more'" (vv. 10–11).

♥ *Grace* met a repentant disciple for breakfast on a beach, then reinstated him to minister to God's people (John 21:1–19). "[Peter] said to [Jesus], 'Lord, You know everything; You know that I love You.' Jesus said to him, 'Feed My sheep'" (v. 17).

♥ *Grace* called murderous Saul out of darkness and into Jesus' piercing light (Acts 9:1–19). "'Saul, Saul, why are you persecuting Me?' And he said, 'Who are You, Lord?' And He said, 'I am Jesus, whom you are persecuting. But rise . . . you will be told what you are to do'" (vv. 4–6).

Did you hear Jesus' voice as He spoke to the adulterous woman? to Peter? to Saul (later known as the apostle Paul)? Do you hear His voice above your own or above those around you who may condemn you for your particular sins? Because you believe in Christ Jesus, you are no longer condemned (Romans 8:1). You "are justified by His grace as a gift, through the redemption that is in Christ Jesus" (Romans 3:24).

While we don't know what came of the forgiven woman, we know Jesus freed her to face the future in faith. Peter and Paul were chosen and emboldened by Jesus to carry the Gospel into the world. By the same grace, Christ calls us, also forgiven followers, and He chooses to work through us too.

While it might be hard to understand God's divine grace, who gets grace? We do!

JOURNAL

Is it difficult for you to wrap your head around grace in its richest meaning? If so, why do you think that is? We may not fully "get" grace, but we get grace: it's ours in Christ! Journal about what that means to you.

PRAYER

Heavenly Father, thank You for revealing Your grace to me in Jesus as I hear You in the Gospel, and as I humbly receive it from You . . .

HAPPY GOOD FRIDAY!

Christ died for our sins in accordance with the Scriptures, . . . He was buried, . . . He was raised on the third day in accordance with the Scriptures. 1 Corinthians 15:3–4

I couldn't beat the blues, but I knew that if I made myself get out of the house, face the sunshine and strong Nebraska wind on that spring day, I would feel better. As I walked into the wind, I started spewing all my frustration and woes to God. I listed several ways that I was failing Him and failing the people around me. I kept circling back to the same thoughts: struggles with certain sins and my failure to move forward or follow through with commitments. I was stuck in the yuck of my poisonous thoughts. But then my cries turned to confession because I knew that the Lord hadn't given up on me. And I knew my sorry heart was just that—sorry. Repentant. (Praise the Lord! The Spirit was moving in me, even on this battle-the-blues day!) As I continued to take *everything* to God, receive His forgiveness, and allow the sunshine to flood my face, I almost missed my friends from church driving by me, trying to get my attention.

You see, it was Good Friday, and the neighborhood children were out of school. These three siblings and their sweet mama waved at me as they pulled into their nearby driveway. They were arriving home from afternoon worship and a grocery run. All of them in turn ran toward me for a hug, hollering, "Happy Good Friday!" on the way. They spoke excitedly of the Run for the Risen Son 5k we were all participating in the next day, and their mama told me that one of them had drawn multiple pictures of the crosses next to an empty tomb. They chatted excitedly, telling me that Easter was coming, and the tomb would be empty!

For the remainder of my walk, my spirits were lifted. My heavy heart was buoyed, and I knew this encounter was not coincidental.

God knew what I needed more than I did, and His answer to my prayer was immediate on that good Good Friday. Had my soul been particularly heavy that day, making me all the more mindful of the sins for which Christ chose to die? of the righteousness that is mine by faith?

[Jesus] Himself bore our sins in His body on the tree, that we might die to sin and live to righteousness. By His wounds you have been healed. (1 Peter 2:24)

I continue to be wowed by God's intimate knowledge of our needs and His saving love for all who believe. Does your heart need to be buoyed by way of His Good News for you? Picture me waving to you today, hollering, "He is risen!" By Jesus' wounds you have been healed.

JOURNAL

What helps buoy your heart when it's heavy? Could walk-and-talk time with the Lord lift your spirits? Praise the Lord as you journal today; He knows your need and He has Good News for you!

PRAYER

Savior Jesus, by Your wounds I am healed. I praise You for saving me, for hearing every prayer as You walk with me too . . .

ALL OR NOTHING

There is therefore now no condemnation for those who are in Christ Jesus. Romans 8:1

I have been known to avoid spaces when they're cluttered because I am distracted by the things that make up the mess and by what they represent: incomplete tasks. I am dismayed by the sight, which leads me to walk in the opposite direction, sometimes giving up on a task entirely. Take my kitchen, for example: when it is mostly clean, I can see clearly how to whip it back into shape. When it's a mess, the goal seems so far away. Overwhelmed, I don't know where to start, so I walk away.

I have an all-or-nothing personality, and I'm not proud of it. I can either be all-in or hands-off about social commitments, work responsibilities, and, yes, household chores. Some parts of my life are in good order, others are messy. Some relationships and responsibilities get messy because I can't give them proper attention, and I'm tempted to give up on them. When something isn't going how I believe it should, I start avoiding it, even if I love it. I procrastinate. Then I catastrophize the situation, certain I've fallen short, let others down, or worse. What if I am a failure?!

Wait! Is this how Jesus sees me?!

Sometimes, life is messy, relationships are messy, and my house is messy. But that doesn't mean I must declare that I am a mess—a failure. Except that—reality check—apart from Christ, I *am*. However, because I am found in Christ and redeemed by Him, I am no longer condemned by my sin (see Romans 8:1). Jesus can take any one of my messes and transform it into a message—*to* me and *through* me to others. He can do immeasurably more by **His miraculous work in me**, by His grace!

What if I consider the things I *am* doing well—in the less-cluttered spaces—and give myself some grace?

Have you found yourself at either of these extremes: feeling good about what you are doing and feeling like you're beyond hope? When you or I fail in any area of our life, Jesus knows. And He doesn't leave us, even if we fail to do our part in daily conversation with Him. He is all-in for you and me. Always. He knows our hearts (and our status) concerning every area of our lives. He holds every piece together (Colossians 1:17), even as He holds us.

Do you avoid cluttered spaces in your life? If so, why do you think that is? What things make up the clutter and what might they represent? In what areas of your life are you procrastinating, if any?

Praise the Lord for His forgiveness in Christ! He meets us where we sit in our struggles, and He covers us with compassion as we rest in His grace and His embrace. The only all-or-nothing that matters is this: I offer nothing for my salvation; Christ has paid it all!

JOURNAL

Resting in God's grace, write about your clutter and choose just one or two things from your list, whether relationships or responsibilities, and give them your attention. The next time you find yourself in this physical or emotional space, there will be one or two fewer procrastinated priorities creating clutter. Give yourself some grace too.

PRAYER

Dear Jesus, thank You for meeting me where I am, with compassion and perfect understanding. In You, there is no condemnation; I rest in Your open arms . . .

BEYOND THE BOUNDS
OF GOD'S GRACE?

Let us then with confidence draw near to the throne of grace, that we may receive mercy and find grace to help in time of need. Hebrews 4:16

What was I thinking?! My cousins and I had a youthful and short-lived fascination with matches and the ability to strike them and create fire. Poof! Such power. Such fun. There was no telling our parents. And no remorse . . . that is, until my father later warned me that one childishly lit match could burn down the farm. *Gulp!* Did I dare confess my former fascination and subsequent misbehavior?

Can you recall a time in your childhood when you did something you knew was wrong but you got away with it . . . and enjoyed it? Maybe only later did you feel remorse for the poor decision you'd made or the wicked thing you'd done. And maybe you were afraid to come clean, to approach your parents in apology, because you were sure that what you'd done was so awful, they wouldn't want to forgive you.

Could those be the thoughts of the prodigal son in the parable Jesus told (recorded in Luke 15)? He was sorry for every wicked thing he had done but wondered how he could hope to approach his father, knowing he was no longer worthy to be called *son* (Luke 15:19). Imagine his surprise and overwhelming joy when he drew near to his childhood home and saw his father running toward him *with open arms*, with a heart fairly bursting with compassion and grace for his beloved son (v. 20).

Jesus' parable reveals the extravagance of our heavenly Father's grace toward us! Despite the many ways we've sinned, from childhood to this very day, our Lord makes us worthy to be called His children because of Jesus' substitutionary sacrifice. Repentant, we can approach God's throne of grace with confidence (Hebrews 4:16). He knows when we are sorry. He runs to us, arms open wide, and forgives us, no matter what sin we've committed or how badly we've messed up. We don't have to fear that our sins have surpassed the bounds of God's immeasurable grace for us in Christ Jesus.

Heavenly Father, thank You for Your forgiveness of _____ from my past.

Father, please also forgive me for _____ today.

As we stand in the shadow of Christ's cross, it's easier to extend grace to others, offering the same forgiveness we freely receive. Maybe a loved one is afraid to come clean to you. Embrace her with open arms, thanking God for the immeasurable extent of His grace and for the same extent of His power at work in you, a conduit of His boundless grace.

JOURNAL

Read Luke 15:11–32, the parable of the prodigal son, and journal your initial takeaways. Write about a time you behaved childishly and later felt remorse. Were you afraid to come clean? To whom can you extend God's grace with open arms today? in the days ahead?

PRAYER

Heavenly Father, thank You for Your saving grace in Jesus . . .

SING A NEW SONG

*Now may our Lord Jesus Christ Himself, and God our Father, who
loved us and gave us eternal comfort and good hope through
grace, comfort your hearts and establish them in every good work
and word. 2 Thessalonians 2:16–17*

I had an awful fight with someone I thought was my friend. Over and over, I recalled her hurtful words. I rehearsed my replies, and although I didn't say the words aloud, the responses I wanted to give her demanded my full attention. Just like that, in a brief moment, I had allowed bitterness to take root, and it was growing and causing trouble where she was concerned. God's commands convicted me:

> See to it that no one fails to obtain the grace of God; that no "root of bitterness" springs up and causes trouble, and by it many become defiled. (Hebrews 12:15)

My bitter thoughts mingled with the sour notes of my rationalization for feeling this way. The resulting mixed melody played like an old, warped LP record, spinning around and around with a distorted sound. With each replay I felt worse. I remembered the Lord's command to take every thought captive and make it obedient to Christ (2 Corinthians 10:5), and God's Word convicted me by the Spirit again:

> Let all bitterness and wrath and anger and clamor and slander be put away from you, along with all malice. Be kind to one another, tenderhearted, forgiving one another, as God in Christ forgave you. (Ephesians 4:31–32)

"As God in Christ forgave you."

God has forgiven me for much more, and He has an incomparably different refrain playing. Do you hear it? Oh, "the immeasurable riches of [God's] grace in kindness toward us in Christ Jesus" (Ephesians 2:7). He can produce grace and kindness in me by His power, enabling me to hand out the same grace I've received so freely, unearned and undeserved. By His great big grace, He can do through me all that I cannot—and would not—on my own. Immeasurably more than I could muster. May the new song that I sing *glorify Him!*

I pray that I tune in to His words of grace and turn up thoughts that are true, honorable, just, pure, lovely, commendable, excellent, and worthy of praise (Philippians 4:8).

Does bitterness try to take root in you? Try this: play God's Word on repeat; even one verse will do. A memorized morsel of God's truth works wonders when your mind is tempted to wander. Sing it aloud, if that helps, when sour notes threaten to surface. Here's a great place to start: "For by grace you have been saved through faith. And this is not your own doing; it is the gift of God" (Ephesians 2:8). May you be an instrument of God's grace!

JOURNAL

Confess bitter notes you have played on repeat, allowing them to take root in you. Forgiven in Christ, sing a new song, tuning in to the words from Philippians 4:8 above, and choosing one of these qualities for the theme of your song.

PRAYER

Dear Lord, by Your power, produce repentance, grace, and kindness in me, enabling me to hand out Your grace as I sing a new song . . .

LIMITLESS

And I pray that you, being rooted and established in love, may have power, together with all the Lord's holy people, to grasp how wide and long and high and deep is the love of Christ, and to know this love that surpasses knowledge—that you may be filled to the measure of all the fullness of God. Ephesians 3:17–19, NIV

I grew up on the Great Plains of South Dakota, where the prairie stretches so wide, you wonder how many miles are contained within a single breathtaking view. Farmland and pastures seem to extend endlessly in every direction, continuing beyond the horizon where the prairie reaches the sky. I know that there's a limit to their length and my eyesight, but to me, the prairie appears to go on forever.

More than just appearing so, we possess something breathtaking that *does* spread forever in every direction: the Lord's limitless grace and love for us in Christ.

[The Lord] does not deal with us according to our sins, nor repay us according to our iniquities. For as high as the heavens are above the earth, so great is His steadfast love toward those who fear Him; as far as the east is from the west, so far does He remove our transgressions from us. (Psalm 103:10–12)

East and west extend infinitely in opposite directions. Let's envision a line with arrows aimed outward at both ends. They never meet. That's how far the Lord has removed our sins from us, and He doesn't "deal with us according to our sins" either (v. 10). In other words, we receive what we don't deserve: His grace. *Only Christ* could pay the cost of our sin by His death. We can't earn His favor or forgiveness either, but we receive it freely. Immeasurable, too, is the height of the heavens above the earth; "so great is His steadfast love" (v. 11).

The opening passage for today's devotion immediately precedes the "immeasurably more" doxology of Ephesians 3:20–21 and provides similar spatial imagery: "how wide and long and high and deep is the love of Christ" (v. 18). Now let's envision lines extending outward four-dimensionally—yes, in every direction! We are rooted, grounded, and established already in His love, and Paul prays that we may have the Holy Spirit's power (v. 16) to comprehend the extent of it, though it exceeds the limits of our intellect or human understanding. We have an amazing juxtaposition before us: by God's work in us by the Spirit, we can know a love that surpasses knowledge. To Him be the glory!

JOURNAL

What other kinds of spatial imagery could help you comprehend the limitless extent of God's love and grace? A view of the ocean? The grains of sand on a beach . . . ?

PRAYER

Holy Spirit, fill me with Your power to know God's love that surpasses knowledge . . .

CHANGELESS TRUTH

The Lord is my strength and my shield; in Him my heart
trusts, and I am helped; my heart exults, and with my song I
give thanks to Him. Psalm 28:7

God's changeless truth prevails in a constantly changing culture.

He is faithful to lead His people through the most difficult circumstances.

I say these scripturally supportive words to myself on repeat, especially when I witness fellow believers facing threats because of their faith . . . and when I read current headlines . . . and as I hear of another heartbreaking atrocity in our broken world . . . and . . . *sigh. God's truth prevails*; He is faithful. And I take comfort as I remember that the Lord is our strength, the One in whom we trust, our protector and provider in whatever comes our way. But sometimes the going gets tough, the narrow road feels rough, and I reason that giving up or walking the way of the world might be the smoother path to trod.

Only in the Lord can I stay the course when culture screams, "Truth is whatever I want it to be!" When the world taunts, "How can an antiquated book speak relevant words to people's needs today?" When skeptics criticize, "Is it really the Word of God anyway?"

My heart is broken over my own sin and that of the world. I want to cry out, "God's Word *is* truth!" It is the only absolute, changeless truth, fully relevant to us today, just as it was when God inspired each writer with every word. Lest someone tells us otherwise, "All Scripture is breathed out by God and profitable for teaching, for reproof, for correction, and for training in righteousness" (2 Timothy 3:16). Jesus, the Word made flesh, is "the way, and the truth, and the life" (John 14:6). And isn't this good, good news?!

God's inerrant, inspired Word is the final authority for our lives, perfectly applicable in our contemporary culture and in every difficult circumstance. We will not always like what God's Word says, so we may be tempted to dismiss some of Scripture because it is not in line with popular thought, opinions of our peers, the dictates of today's culture, or the choices we make in our own circumstances. But God's changeless truth prevails; He calls us to live in obedience to His Word, which tells us not to be conformed to this world but, rather, to be transformed in Christ so that we may know God's will (Romans 12:2).

Praise God! By His grace, He picks us up when we stumble in obedience to Him and every time we have chosen the so-called smoother path of the world. We come to Him with repentant hearts, confident that we receive His forgiveness in Christ. We trust in our strength and our shield, and we are helped. We give thanks for His power at work in us, enabling us to stay the course and stand firm in the truth.

JOURNAL

What cultural mantras do you hear that seek to challenge God's changeless truth? Write out supportive words based on Scripture or verses you can say on repeat when you need a comforting reminder of God's truth.

PRAYER

Lord, I know that You can do immeasurably more than all I ask or imagine, as You work through me, enabling me to stand in Your truth. Help me stay the course . . .

GRACIOUS WORDS

Walk in wisdom toward outsiders, making the best use of the time. Let your speech always be gracious, seasoned with salt, so that you may know how you ought to answer each person. Colossians 4:5–6

I was tired. It was an I've-traveled-for-a-solid-month degree of tired. Usually I love interacting with people and eagerly anticipate meeting my next new friend, but that evening, I didn't have much left to give.

I had just wrapped up my fourth retreat in a row, and as I boarded my final flight, I chose the first open aisle seat. An elderly man had already buckled himself into the window seat, and we gave each other polite smiles and nods. When a woman chose the seat between us, I was secretly grateful that she kept to herself. Before long, however, she was on the receiving end of an earful from the man in the window seat that continued throughout the flight. She kindly nodded and provided one-word responses as he poured out a plethora of accomplishments, adventures, and boastings. I rested with my eyes closed, pleased that I had avoided this conversation.

When the plane landed and we were waiting to deboard, the girl sitting directly in front of the chatty man unbuckled her seat belt and turned around to face him, kneeling in her seat. Immediately, they engaged in friendly banter. She'd heard his stories throughout the flight and was fascinated by them. She wanted him to know her adventures too; this sweet girl was excited to make a new friend in the limited time we had left together.

My thoughts, I'm embarrassed to say, had gone a different direction than hers had during that flight. This girl's gracious thoughts toward a stranger gave way to words that were seasoned with salt. I don't know if she shared her faith that day, but her winsome smile and kind words were Christlike. I deboarded the plane praying for forgiveness for my negative thoughts and thanking God for the lesson I learned from a little girl. I asked myself, *What does it look like to "walk in wisdom," whether I'm seated beside a fellow believer or someone who hasn't yet met Jesus?*

Maybe this girl was looking for answers and didn't even know it. Maybe the man would have been blessed by some salty speech from me. Do I shy away from words with a stranger when I worry what they might say or decide that I don't have the energy? One thing's for sure: by God's grace, I can be prepared to give an answer if they ask me for the reason (Jesus!) for the hope that I have (1 Peter 3:15).

Figuratively speaking, who's in a seat adjacent to you? Maybe all you have to do is turn to see them. *Ask God* for renewed energy when you've little left to give. Expect Him to do immeasurably more through you, even when your time and energy are limited, as He equips you to make the most of that opportunity and works through you to accomplish His will. With excitement like that little girl's, you can listen with genuine interest. You might receive an earful. And who knows? You may get to share your adventures in Christ too.

JOURNAL

Do you avoid conversations with strangers or are you eager to engage with them? Maybe it depends on the day. Regardless, consider ways you may prepare to "walk in wisdom" beside someone new. Who's seated near you?

PRAYER

Dear God, give me a heart for future friends who may be adjacent to me today. Renew my energy so I make the most of the time . . .

LIVING WATER

Whoever drinks of the water that I will give him will never be thirsty again. The water that I will give him will become in him a spring of water welling up to eternal life. John 4:14

Thirst-quenching. Cold, clean, bottled water had never tasted so good. I had just trudged past the finish line of the half-marathon with the knowledge that I had not adequately hydrated that morning. I was afraid I would have to stop at the dreaded porta-potties along the way, so I steered clear of water before the race. Nearing mile ten with three more to go, I began to experience weakness and lethargy that I hadn't felt before, even during my training leading up to this race. Still, I crossed the finish line on my feet. A bottle of water was thrust into my shaking hand, and I swallowed it all at once, the way one might picture a parched traveler in the desert after she's crawled to an oasis. My thirst was finally quenched, several hours and several bottles of water later.

Our bodies require regular hydration; after all, *by God's design* water makes up roughly 60 percent of our body weight. We will thirst again and again because we receive only temporary satisfaction for our ongoing need. This continual thirst stands in sharp contrast to the thirst Jesus addresses when He confronts the Samaritan woman at the well:

> Whoever drinks of the water that I will give him will never be thirsty again. The water that I will give him will become in him a spring of water welling up to eternal life. (John 4:14)

Living water. Salvation. Eternal life. The gift of God in Jesus Christ, by His grace through faith.

In Baptism, God miraculously works faith in our hearts by the power of the Holy Spirit through water connected to His living Word. We are quenched by the God-breathed words of Scripture proclaiming Christ's redeeming grace, flowing into us as we drink of it. Only Christ can satisfy our thirst for salvation—our need for a Savior. In this sense, we will never thirst again. But in our daily walk, we face challenges that drain us, from struggles with health to strains in a relationship, from conflicts at church to trials or tragedy in the world at large.

Weak, stumbling, and shaking, we come to Christ, ready to receive spiritual replenishment. We draw on His strength as we receive His Holy Supper during worship, and when we drink from His Word as it's read, taught, proclaimed, and shared.

As you soak up God's Word and call upon Him in prayer, He fills you . . . and then He sends you out, in the Spirit's power! By your words and by the work of your hands, the world will know that you have been quenched by His redeeming grace, that Christ lives in you.

In Him we live and move and have our being. (Acts 17:28)

Others who are parched and looking for lasting hydration are quenched by His grace as it's shared through you, a wellspring of the Father's love.

JOURNAL	PRAYER
Sometimes we are physically dehydrated and don't even know it. Compare this with spiritual dehydration. When have you noticed that you were parched during your faith walk?	Dear God, I praise You for the living water I have in Jesus! Fill me through Your Word today; only You can satiate my thirst . . .

ORDINARY DAYS, EXTRAORDINARY GRACE

So if there is any encouragement in Christ, any comfort from love, any participation in the Spirit, any affection and sympathy, complete my joy by being of the same mind, having the same love, being in full accord and of one mind. Philippians 2:1–2

Have you ever had one of those days when you wonder if anything you've done makes a difference? Everything is so very . . . ordinary. Routine. But did you know that even (maybe especially) on ordinary days, we get to practice becoming more like Jesus?! We can respond in obedience, by God's grace, as He continuously transforms us into the image of Christ (2 Corinthians 3:18) as *He works in us by the Spirit*.

I recall one ordinary day that included a couple of phone calls from friends, a few texts from my kids, a trip to the grocery store, email replies, a chat with my husband over dinner, and devotion time alone. I was tempted to wonder how God could be shaping or stretching me into Christlikeness on such an ordinary day. But, wait. I reviewed my day again, this time from another angle. Through the rhetorical words of Philippians 2:1–2, I saw that Christ provided in specific ways on this average day, by His grace.

- ♥ *Comfort* and *sympathy* in my phone conversations with those friends; I gave and received some of both, in Christ's love.

- ♥ *Participation in the Spirit* as I sent up specific prayers my children requested, and again as I received the good Word from God during my devotions, which nourished my soul and provided direction for the day.

- ♥ *Encouragement* in my conversation with the checker on the other side of the conveyor belt. (She said the florals on my purse literally brightened her day, and we both giggled! I asked God to bless her day, and she responded with a smile.)

💜 *Affection* during conversation with my husband as we nourished our bodies and our relationship over the simple dinner I had made.

I can trust that God used my humble offerings in each of these opportunities to do immeasurably more, by His grace, for me and for those I interacted with. Do I have room to grow? Absolutely! Did I miss some opportunities to share Christ in my interactions on this ordinary day? Yes. Am I a work in progress? God says so:

He who began a good work in you will bring it to completion at the day of Jesus Christ. (Philippians 1:6)

By His extraordinary grace, He will give me new opportunities tomorrow, and He will do the same for you. So, I'm going to thank Him for the next ordinary day . . . and the next. Ordinary days provide opportunities to be transformed by an extraordinary Savior, to grow in the same love for others that He has for you and me.

JOURNAL

Write about an ordinary day and the opportunities God provided for you to practice Christlikeness and live out your witness for Him. In what tangible ways will you practice it today, guided by His extraordinary grace?

PRAYER

Dear Lord, open my eyes on ordinary days to see the opportunities in front of me. Embolden me to share Your extraordinary grace as I grow in the same love for others that You have for me . . .

IMMEASURABLY MORE
Love

TREASURED POSSESSION

The Lord has chosen you to be a people for His treasured possession. Deuteronomy 14:2

Priceless. Treasured. Precious. We save these words for our very favorite things, don't we? Time with loved ones. Milestone moments and memories. Unforgettable gifts. But will we willingly look in the mirror and speak these same words as descriptions of our worth? *Priceless. Treasured. Precious.* These are but a few of the many words we could use to describe the measure of our worth to our Maker and Redeemer, and our identity is found in Him!

The One who knit you together in your mother's womb (Psalm 139:13) also spared no expense to purchase you back, to redeem you from your sin. "You were bought with a price" (1 Corinthians 6:20), the ultimate price of Christ's life. *Salvation is your most unforgettable gift.* God's words through the prophet Isaiah speak to us today:

> I have redeemed you; I have called you by name, you are Mine. . . . You are precious in My eyes, and honored, and I love you. (Isaiah 43:1, 4)

You and I get to call the one true God "Abba! Father!" (Romans 8:15). He has chosen us as His beloved children (Ephesians 5:1) in Christ Jesus.

God inspired writers across Scripture with every word. And they used endearing descriptions of love through word pictures that reveal the measure of His love for us. God's love is greater than the love of a mother who would not forget the child nursing at her breast (Isaiah 49:15). Even greater than the love a bridegroom has, rejoicing over his bride on their wedding day (Isaiah 62:5). As a hen who longs to gather her brood under her wings (Luke 13:34). And in Jesus' own words, the love that would lead someone to sacrifice his life for the friend he loves (John 15:13).

With every depiction, we see glimpses of God's great love that is both tender and joyful. Both protective and sacrificial. He spared nothing to claim you as His own treasured possession. He knows your name; you are precious in His sight. Can you believe it?! It's true. God loves you immeasurably more than you could hope, ask, or imagine, and He works lovingly in you today, by the Spirit, empowering you to treasure others the same way!

JOURNAL

Look in the mirror and tell your reflection, this precious person, what God says about her. (Go ahead.) Write the words you chose. Draw a picture or write a word cloud picture (an image composed of words related to that image) that may help you envision the measure of God's love for you.

PRAYER

Dear heavenly Father, thank You for choosing me in Christ to be Your beloved child. Help me remember my worth in You . . .

SACRIFICIAL LOVE

Christ loved us and gave Himself up for us, a fragrant offering and
sacrifice to God. Ephesians 5:2

For centuries, God's people brought burnt offerings before the Lord to
atone for their sins. As the smoke rose from these regular sacrifices, it was
a pleasing aroma—a "fragrant offering"—to the Lord because it was offered
with repentance and in faith. Death was necessary to pay the price for sin,
and God allowed for the substitutionary sacrifice of the animal in the place
of His people. But one of these sacrifices was never enough. Then Christ
came to fulfill what only the sinless Son of God could. He became for us the
one final sacrifice for the complete atonement of our sins. Hebrews 10:12
proclaims, "Christ . . . offered for all time a single sacrifice for sins."

While there are four Greek words for our one English word *love, agape*
is the Greek word used to define God's perfect love for us that is both self-
giving and sacrificial. In love, God came down to us in His Son, the promised Messiah, our Savior. *There is no greater love!* Jesus Himself said,

Greater love has no one than this, that someone lay down his life for his
friends. (John 15:13)

At the heart of our Christian faith is Jesus' death and resurrection. This
monumental act revealed fully the immeasurable love of God, who gave us
everything when He gave up His Son. He sacrificed Himself in our place as
punishment for our sins, and He rose victorious, saving us for eternity.

Love *gives*.

For God so loved the world that He gave . . . (John 3:16)

So begins the most well-known verse in Scripture. Sacrificial love
gives without expecting anything in return. How can we give as He gave?
Jesus said,

This is My commandment, that you love one another as I have loved you. (John 15:12)

In Christian love for others, we're called to show others preference, to place their needs ahead of our own, as God did for us in Christ. He knew our greatest need was a Savior, and Christ's love flowing to us frees and emboldens us to meet the needs of one another. We are the vessel through which His love is poured out. By His power flowing through us, we can honor and esteem others, serving them in sacrificial love too. Paul exhorted his fellow believers to "present your bodies as a living sacrifice, holy and acceptable to God, which is your spiritual worship" (Romans 12:1).

Become a student of those you serve; seek to recognize their greatest needs and work to meet them. To whom will you commit your time and your life, whatever the cost? Trust God to do immeasurably more through your sacrificial acts of love than you could ask or imagine.

JOURNAL

List some ways you can sacrifice your time for the sake of someone. How can you be mindful of his or her needs? What might it look like to give, even if it means you receive less or go without?

PRAYER

Dear Jesus, I praise You for the fragrant offering You made, sacrificing Yourself in my place. Make my life a pleasing aroma of sacrificial service . . .

APPLE OF HIS EYE

Keep me as the apple of Your eye. Psalm 17:8

"That little princess is the apple of her grandpa's eye!" One glance at Grandpa's beaming smile, and you know it's true, even if you don't really understand the expression.

In Psalm 17, King David does more than just ask God to keep an eye on him; David longs to be in the center of God's gaze. This simple expression refers to the effect of looking someone in the eye at point-blank range. If the light is just right, you will see an image of yourself reflected in the eye of that person. Do you know what this means? Your reflection is found in the gaze of the Father. *You are the apple of God's eye.* The Creator who formed you in His image, who fearfully and wonderfully made you (Psalm 139:14), says you are His workmanship—His masterpiece—created in Christ Jesus (Ephesians 2:10), and His loving gaze is always upon you.

> The LORD bless you and keep you; the LORD make His face shine on you and be gracious to you; the LORD turn His face toward you and give you peace. (Numbers 6:24–26, NIV)

Not only does the Lord keep you in the center of His vision, but His face shines on you (like Grandpa's beaming smile, only greater). Sister in Christ, this is an image of delight! Your Savior's face turns toward you with whole-hearted devotion and attention. His grace and peace in Christ rests upon you too. Moses received these words of blessing from the Lord for Aaron to speak over God's chosen people, the Israelites. Thousands of years later, God's chosen people in Christ receive the same words of benediction at the close of many worship services. The same loving Lord looks upon us today.

As imitators of God (Ephesians 5:1) and with His mighty work within us, we look on others with the same love. Gaze with love upon those God has placed beside you on your path, in your home, and all within viewing range.

Let the light of Christ shine through you as you delight in someone today, as you give them your devotion and undivided attention and offer them the same grace and peace in Christ that God first gave you.

JOURNAL

Read Zephaniah 3:17 and share what ways God delights over you in this passage. Write about someone within your viewing range. Consider what way you can delight in this person today.

PRAYER

Dear Lord God, keep me as the apple of Your eye; shine Your face upon me and let me look on others with the same love . . .

ABIDE

[Jesus said,] "As the Father has loved Me, so have I loved you. Abide in My love." John 15:9

Have you ever felt like you were all alone in the middle of a crowd? Sometimes my loneliest seasons haven't been ones of physical isolation, but when I was lonely for other reasons. When I feel like I'm on an island because I have no one to talk to or because I feel like no one would understand, I return to this truth about God's love for me in Christ: He abides with me. He tells me to abide in His love. So, I've sought, by His grace, to remain mindful of His continual presence.

Have you ever felt so alone that you wondered if even God was with you? Take comfort in King David's words when he proclaimed there was nowhere that he could go where God was not present. This is true for you too: by His hand He leads you; His right hand holds yours (see Psalm 139:7–10). He will never leave your side (Hebrews 13:5).

> By this we know that we abide in Him and He in us, because He has given us of His Spirit. . . . Whoever confesses that Jesus is the Son of God, God abides in him, and he in God. So we have come to know and to believe the love that God has for us. God is love, and whoever abides in love abides in God, and God abides in him. (1 John 4:13, 15–16)

Abide. That's what He does. Other translations state: Remain. Stay. Live. Continue. He abides with you right now as you read these words. He remains with me, even after I write them. He lives in you and me by the power of the Holy Spirit. Whether you're surrounded by others or all alone, God is always approachable because *He is always present!* Engage in dialogue or sit in silence, confident that He continues to abide with you.

> If we love one another, God abides in us and His love is perfected in us. (1 John 4:12)

You and I love because He first loved us. By His abiding presence and power in us, we can be conduits of His love, reaching out in His name, and all the while trusting His transformative work in us to make us more like Jesus. Where will we "show up" for the sake of someone's good? How can we draw close enough to hold her hands—in her pain and in her joy? We can live out the Gospel in love as we abide with others.

For I, the LORD your God, hold your right hand; it is I who say to you, "Fear not, I am the one who helps you." (Isaiah 41:13)

Whose hand will you hold, abiding in love as your Father abides with you?

JOURNAL

Write about a time when your abiding presence with a friend, loved one, or coworker spoke more clearly than words could. Who could use a gentle reminder that she is never alone because of the abiding love of Christ?

PRAYER

Lord God, thank You for Your abiding love for me. Show me whose hands I can hold as You hold mine . . .

BROWN EYES

Are not five sparrows sold for two pennies? And not one of them is forgotten before God. Why, even the hairs of your head are all numbered. Fear not; you are of more value than many sparrows. Luke 12:6–7

My husband, Cory, dragged that stuffed bear everywhere. I heard stories about his beloved Brown Eyes long before I laid eyes on his childhood companion. When my mother-in-law sent a tub full of childhood treasures to us, there was Brown Eyes, much to Cory's delight. What did I see? Matted and missing fur, loose stitching, dark stains, and missing eyes. Brown Eyes wasn't created that way; long ago, he was whole and clean. He only became ragged with wear and tear and time. But "ragged" is not his identity. He may be unlovely to look at now, but he is not unloved. Cory gazes at Brown Eyes with a love that sees beyond its ragged appearance. He deems Brown Eyes treasured and precious, no matter what anyone else thinks. He loves that bear just because it belongs to him.

Do you question your value? Have you stared at your flaws, inside or out, and wondered what could possibly make you lovable or valuable? In Luke 12:6–7, Jesus comforted and encouraged His disciples with a story that revealed the *measure of their worth to Him*. He knew they would understand the insignificance of a sparrow to the world around them, yet God loved these little birds, remembering every one of them. (Even today, the sparrow is known to be the most abundant bird in the world, with an estimated population of 1.6 billion. God remembers every one of them too.) Jesus reassured His disciples that God's love for His people was immeasurably greater.

Anyone else might take one look at that old bear and toss it in the trash. But not the one who loves it. Brown Eyes is invaluable in Cory's eyes. Although someone may decide you're worthless, God says otherwise, and His voice is the only one that matters. His love for you gives you full value and worth. Nothing you have done (or failed to do), no matter how tattered or torn you've become, whatever wear you've sustained, your value can never be lessened or diminished in Christ.

God came to us when we were quite ragged and unlovable, stained in sin. He demonstrated His immeasurable love for us: while sinners, Jesus died for us (Romans 5:8). Covered in Christ, you and I are made brand new, like ole' Brown Eyes when Cory received him as a child.

We are not only God's treasured and precious possession, but we are also valuable vessels, "stuffed" with the Spirit, for present and future purposes far greater than we can imagine.

JOURNAL

What have you owned that has little to no value to anyone else but is a treasured possession to you? How can you relate this to your worth in God's eyes? "Stuffed" with the Spirit, ponder His future purposes for you.

PRAYER

Lord God, thank You for making me brand new in Christ . . .

UNCONDITIONAL

*See what great love the Father has lavished on us, that we should be
called children of God! And that is what we are! 1 John 3:1, NIV*

I led a recent women's retreat on the topic of God's unconditional love
and grace. As I wrapped up a session, I offered time for comments or questions. A young woman spoke up courageously. She admitted through tears
that while she knew all about grace, until that day, she had not grasped the
extent of God's grace for her. She had secretly believed there were conditions to it—a limit to the extent of His love—and that she'd passed the limit.
She'd held onto shame, believing that God couldn't continue to love and
forgive her because of her ongoing struggle to forgive someone else. She
boldly shared that she finally felt free! She learned anew that God's love for
her in Christ is immeasurably greater than her sin. It is truly unconditional.

I've seen invisible weights lifted off women as we uncover this truth
together in God's Word. Maybe they've heard the Gospel most of their
lives, and while they believe it, they've fallen for the lie that somewhere or
somehow, they've sinned beyond the reaches of God's love.

Romans 5:5 tells us, "God's love has been poured into our hearts
through the Holy Spirit." But maybe we don't feel loved or lovable. Perhaps
we have fallen for the lie that we must earn God's love or mistakenly believe
that His love has limits or conditions.

God's love knows no limits and has no end. We cannot earn it and don't
deserve it, but *He lavishes it upon us anyway!* We are His chosen children
in Christ (1 John 3:1). While our feelings may betray us, God's perfect Word
never will. There we read that He so loved us that He gave His Son (John
3:16), who poured out His life for our sins, reconciled us to our Creator, and
gave us eternal life. Nothing we do or fail to do can nullify God's unconditional love for us!

Weight lifted, you are free to love others in the same way! Consider the
immeasurable ways God may work through you to extend His love to others,

even if you receive nothing from them in return. By His grace, you can love even when it's undeserved; you can love without limits or conditions.

Maybe you're thinking, "But what about that person (with whom you struggle)?" It can help to remember who and whose you are. Although you were formerly separated from God by your sin, you're a new creation in Christ (2 Corinthians 5:17). Knowing your true identity and worth may enable you to look at conflict in a new light as you ask yourself, "Who am I? A child of God, unconditionally loved. Who is that person? Also someone for whom Christ died."

What words or verses could help you remember the truth of His unconditional, lavish love for you?

JOURNAL

Recall a time of conflict or disagreement with a friend or loved one. Write a prayer, surrendering it to God. Ask for His grace to forgive; to love in spite of . . . in the midst of . . . no matter what. Insert the same name(s) on each blank in the prayer and talk to the Lord.

PRAYER

God, help me to view myself and _____ as You view both of us, with unconditional love. Forgive me for being critical of _____, another person for whom Christ died . . .

JUST LIKE YOU!

Therefore be imitators of God, as beloved children. And walk in love, as Christ loved us and gave Himself up for us. Ephesians 5:1–2

Did you know that the word *Christian* can be defined as "little Christ"? When I read this definition, I envision a little child following in the footsteps of her daddy, mimicking his every move. "I want to be just like you when I grow up, Daddy!" she squeals, aspiring to speak, live, and love just as she sees her daddy doing. Even the best daddies and mommies, no matter how imitation-worthy, can't hold a candle to our loving Lord, whose walk is perfect, whose ways are pure and holy.

Although once lost in sin, we have been *chosen by God* in Christ, who "loved us and gave Himself up for us," so that we, now found and free, can walk in the same love, following in His footsteps, imitating Him at every turn. And as we go, bolstered by His strength, we can trust Him to do far more abundantly through us than we could ever imagine (or accomplish on our own, if that were even possible), to the glory of God.

Imitating God means living a life of love and grace, forgiving undeserving sinners as He forgave us (also undeserving sinners) through Christ's cross, and walking in the same kind of love Christ has for us. In Greek, *walk* (*peripateo*) means "to live; to follow." As imitators, we follow after the One we hope to emulate. The apostle Paul exhorts us,

Be imitators of me, as I am of Christ. (1 Corinthians 11:1)

I am married to a man who walks in love, truly seeking to imitate his Savior, by His grace. So often, Cory sacrifices for me, for the beloved people of our church, and for his many loved ones. I witness his love in action as He provides for the spiritual needs of those entrusted to his care. He makes middle-of-the-night hospital runs, reaches out to hurting people, and extends grace and a helping hand to those who are often overlooked. I hear him humbly pray for a walk that imitates his Lord and Savior, and I see evidence of his imitations every day.

Maybe my husband's example has you thinking of Christ-imitators around you. Thank them for their humble actions and prayerfully seek to imitate what you see in them, that God may be glorified in you too.

JOURNAL

Take a good look around you. Who is imitating Jesus and in what ways? How is God glorified? What specific way do you want to imitate Him today?

PRAYER

Dear God, I want to follow Your footsteps, walking in sacrificial love for others. May they see You in me . . .

ENDURING AND ETERNAL

But the steadfast love of the Lord is from everlasting to everlasting on those who fear Him. Psalm 103:17

"All good things must come to an end." Too many times I hear people say this and sigh. And I get it. I don't want good things to end, do you? I've lamented the end of a feel-good movie, the bottom of a bowl of cherry chocolate chip ice cream, and the last day of a vacation. But must all good things come to an end? Only a few things are truly end*less*. Enduring. Eternal. (And the best definition of *good*!) They include God's love for you in Christ Jesus and your life in Christ, by God's grace through faith!

God spoke through the prophet Jeremiah,

I have loved you with an everlasting love; therefore I have continued My faithfulness to you. (Jeremiah 31:3)

Faithful is who God is and love is what He gives, eternally. And who are we? We are solely defined by His everlasting love for us in Christ Jesus, lover of our souls and Savior of our sins. Our identity is rooted and complete in Him; our value is measured by the eternal nature of His love too. Who we are is really *whose* we are; *we belong to Him.*

Do you need to receive this reassurance again . . . and again? Turn to Psalm 136 and read the refrain, "For His steadfast love endures forever," at the end of all twenty-six verses, every verse flowing with thanks and praise. You'll find this phrase in many other places too. *Steadfast love* is one word in Hebrew, *hesed,* and is unique to the Hebrew language. So rich in meaning, *hesed* speaks of God's loving kindness, His eternal faithfulness and favor, His abundance of love and mercy, and more.

Write your name on every line as you read: God loves _____ with an everlasting love and is forever faithful to _____ (Jeremiah 31:3). Absolutely nothing can separate _____ from His love in Christ (Romans 8:39)! By the power of His Spirit in _____, Christ dwells in _____'s heart through faith, that _____ may have strength to comprehend how great His love is for _____, which surpasses knowledge (Ephesians 3:16–19). In God's love for _____, He sent His Son to die in _____'s place, that _____ may have eternal life in Him (John 3:16).

In what ways can you express your love today? Trust God to do immeasurably more through you than you can ask or think when you share His enduring, eternal love with someone else.

Remember all those good things we wish wouldn't end? Praise God that none compare with the few things that endure . . . forever!

JOURNAL

Share God's enduring love today. Make a simple list of ideas: for example, give someone your time and listen well. Pray with a friend throughout her struggle. Write a note with a reminder of who (and whose!) she is and how much she is loved.

PRAYER

Lord, Your love never ends! Help me remember who and whose I am in Christ . . .

OVERFLOW

That you, being rooted and grounded in love, may have strength
to comprehend with all the saints what is the breadth and
length and height and depth, and to know the love of Christ
that surpasses knowledge, that you may be filled with all the
fullness of God. Ephesians 3:17–19

Close your eyes and try to envision the limitless breadth, length, height, and depth of Christ's love for you. What does it look like? Like a cup running over in every direction? Like the expanse of the ocean and the height of the sky? Although we cannot possibly grasp the extent of God's abundant, limitless love in Christ, we receive the full measure of it! We are rooted and grounded in it *and* we are filled to overflowing with it. We learn more of His love and grow in it as we walk in His Word. There, we learn His heart for us, His thoughts of us, and His promises for us in Christ—for today and for eternity.

And it is my prayer that your love may abound more and more, with knowledge and all discernment, so that you may approve what is excellent, and so be pure and blameless for the day of Christ, filled with the fruit of righteousness that comes through Jesus Christ, to the glory and praise of God. (Philippians 1:9–11)

Filled with Christ's righteousness, we are able to love as He does. To abound is to have *in abundance*, right? Synonymous with *overflowing*, this is the measure of love that Paul prays the believers have for one another. And not just overflowing, as it already is, but "more and more," ever-growing! Paul prays that their love would only continue to increase, Christ working in them.

May the Lord make you increase and abound in love for one another and for all. (1 Thessalonians 3:12)

By His grace, we can abound in love for fellow believers . . . and for all. All? *Gulp*. Even the unlovely woman who hurls insults in our direction? The misguided people in our midst who reject Christ and mistreat us? The family whose culture and values are so different from ours? You and I are to love all of these? Yes, and this is possible only because He first loved us (1 John 4:19). The Gospel frees us and the Holy Spirit empowers us to share the love of Christ—the same love He first poured into us!

JOURNAL

Draw or write about the overflow as you envision the measure of God's love for you. What's one way you can extend God's love to someone who has been difficult to love?

PRAYER

Lord God, I praise You for Your overflowing love for me in Christ. Forgive me for my failure to love all as You do. Move in me, Holy Spirit, to increase and abound in love for

_____ . . .

WHO'S TO JUDGE?

How can you say to your brother, "Brother, let me take out the
speck that is in your eye," when you yourself do not see the log that
is in your own eye? You hypocrite, first take the log out of your
own eye, and then you will see clearly to take out the speck that is
in your brother's eye. Luke 6:42

How quickly I judge someone, then justify my judgment because that person's behavior is negatively impacting me. What if her choices are harmful to herself too? I seek God's direction, asking, "When is this concern valid?" When does this person need some attention or grace or gentle words of correction? Judgment is for God alone to exact, according to His righteousness. Loving her is my first priority, and with God's help by the Spirit, my judgy feelings fade.

I consider my own struggles with sin and how I'd feel if my sins were used to define me. So, I seek to apply that mindset to others. May I meet each person where he is, show him genuine love, and trust God to keep working in him as He works in me. I can trust the Lord to do immeasurably more than I may ask or think, according to the *limitless measure of His love* for both of us and His power within us too.

Love also acts for the good of others. Recently I've seen the first half of Luke 6:42 quoted to justify why we should not judge others. (After all, who are we to judge our brother's speck when we're dealing with our own log, right?) While that's true, we need to look with scrutiny at the continuation of Jesus' words in the second half of the same verse.

In deep humility, we recognize and repent of our own misgivings before we can seek to help another. Paul exhorts us,

With all humility and gentleness, with patience, [bear] with one another
in love. (Ephesians 4:2)

If we're to admonish our brother or sister, we do so gently, with patience . . . in love. Only in sincere love for our fellow believers can we help them. This is not judging; this is love in action for their good and for God's glory, in the light of His grace. May we not turn a blind eye to our loved ones' struggles with sin. May we "keep loving one another earnestly, since love covers a multitude of sins" (1 Peter 4:8).

If your brother sins, rebuke him, and if he repents, forgive him. (Luke 17:3)

Brothers, if anyone is caught in any transgression, you who are spiritual should restore him in a spirit of gentleness. (Galatians 6:1)

Love Himself acted for our greatest good, with the utmost gentleness, patience, and care. He demonstrated His immeasurable love for us in this: "While we were still sinners, Christ died for us" (Romans 5:8).

JOURNAL	PRAYER
When have you placed yourself in the judgment seat meant only for God? In what ways may you be able to help out of love for another's good, after humbly confessing your own sin?	Dear Lord God, forgive me for being quick to judge. Only in Your strength may I remove the log in my eye. Give me grace to help my brother and sister with their specks . . .

IMMEASURABLY MORE
Power

ROUGH ROADS

Great is our Lord, and abundant in power; His understanding is beyond measure. Psalm 147:5

I pray that my words spoke hope to a friend whose family was on a rough and rocky road. When we met over coffee, my friend told me they were shaken, and the path wasn't going to get smoother any time soon. As she spoke with a vulnerability that revealed her trust in me, I wanted to honor that trust by listening well. This trial was testing her faith, and a jumbled mix of emotions left her feeling inadequate. I knew I couldn't fix her situation or take away the pain, and I didn't want to blurt out an insensitive "I understand" when I have not traveled the same rough road. I prayed for discernment: when to listen and when to speak, then I vulnerably shared about my own walk down a rough road.

During that time, I had felt like a fraud, behaving like a strong spiritual leader but struggling inside to trust God. I was ashamed to think that now that my time of tribulation had come, I had failed some kind of test. Only much later, when I looked back on that difficult journey, could I see with clarity that my Savior not only held me up but also gave me bravery in it, although I hadn't recognized it at the time. I learned that my response to difficulty was never about my own strength or ability; it was about Jesus, His power, and *His faithfulness to carry me every step of the way* when I had nothing to give and no answers, only a fledgling faith.

My Savior did not let go of me, even when I had no strength to hold onto Him. He covered my inadequacy with His sufficiency (2 Corinthians

12:9). He completes what I lack. And I could tell my friend that He does the same for her. He understands our jumbled mix of feelings; He holds us in our pain, amidst every rocky step and every shaky circumstance. He forgives us wherever we fall short. He is "abundant in power; His understanding is beyond measure."

I could speak God's truth to my friend, and I believe that God used my humble words and my extension of His grace for far more. I trust Him at His Word, believing that He is able to do far more abundantly than all we ask or imagine, according to the power—His power—at work in us (Ephesians 3:20). The measure of His work exceeds our wildest imagination!

JOURNAL

What honest, even vulnerable, words can you offer to someone who is going down a rough road? Maybe you've walked a rocky road too. Who needs a friend to listen? To remind her that God is all powerful to hear and help her too?

PRAYER

Lord God, by Your mighty power, use my words to speak Your grace to someone walking a rough road . . .

SEASONAL GROWTH

*For everything there is a season, and a time for every matter
under heaven. Ecclesiastes 3:1*

With each turning season of the year I find myself a bit melancholy, sad that the former season has passed (especially when winter is on its way!), as I wonder what the next season will hold. By God's design, the changing of the seasons provides a time for planting, a time for growth, a time for harvest, and a time for rest, but what if we apply the word *season* to life? Then *every* season is a time for growth. Growth is good, and who doesn't want to keep growing in some (or several) ways? Recently, I made a list of goals for growth, personally and spiritually. By God's grace, I want to

- grow in faith and wisdom.
- grow in discernment of the Holy Spirit's work.
- grow in skills that serve my neighbor.
- grow in relationship with Jesus and with others.

(That's a lot of directions and aspirations for growth in my Savior's strength!) But growth often happens within seasons of strife, difficulty, and challenge too. Growth can happen amidst a battle and even as a result of pruning. It's no wonder we have the phrase *growing pains*.

I want to rush through a season of sadness to a season of joy, but what if both emotions are found within the same season? Maybe there is a purpose for the unlikely coupling of these mixed emotions when they are the result of mixed circumstances, mixed opportunities, and a mix of open and closed doors . . . even a mix of strong and struggling relationships.

Perhaps a portion of our lives remains comfortable and familiar while another portion is so new that we're still discovering and learning about it. Our shortsightedness could keep us from recognizing that yesterday's unique mix brought us to today, readying us for what will come our way.

And today, with its potential mix of light and heavy details, will prepare us for tomorrow as the Holy Spirit produces growth in us, sometimes without our recognizing it right away. Thank God for His forgiveness of our poor vision and lack of recognition, for new sight and a new day . . . and growth along the way.

Only an all-wise, all-powerful God could orchestrate every intricate detail in every season to bring about growth and good for His glory. In every mix may we remember we serve a mighty God who is able to do immeasurably more than all we ask of Him, *according to His power at work in us by the Holy Spirit* (Ephesians 3:20). Maybe His current work in you will enable you to step into the next season with a new skill, deeper wisdom, and stronger faith for the plans He has in store.

May we see both the beauty and the difficulty, the sameness and the changes in every season . . . and recognize His hand in it, always and only for good.

JOURNAL

Make a list of personal and spiritual goals for growth, and pray for the Spirit to guide every goal. Write about growing pains you've experienced and the good that has blossomed as a result.

PRAYER

Dear Lord God, guide me by Your strength throughout every season of growth, according to Your Word and wisdom . . .

ALL-POWERFUL

Be strong in the Lord and in the strength of His might. Ephesians 6:10

The slower-paced, seemingly mundane seasons of our lives are not any less Spirit-filled than times of growth. God is not working any less often or any less mightily in these seasons than when we're having regular ah-ha's or seeing recognizable transformation. May we choose, by God's grace, to grow in His Word and in prayer during all such seasons. And may we not berate ourselves during the doldrums or less-spectacular seasons, thinking that our actions cause God to work any less powerfully; that by our lack of action, He would fail to protect or provide for us. By His grace for us in Jesus, we can trust that He is at work even when we're not feeling it, and we are growing as *we receive all that we need from Him* in Word and worship and through edifying relationships with fellow believers.

May we also recognize when such a season includes spiritual attack, remembering that the evil one is real.

> For we do not wrestle against flesh and blood, but against the rulers, against the authorities, against the cosmic powers over this present darkness, against the spiritual forces of evil in the heavenly places. (Ephesians 6:12)

Sometimes a mundane season turns into a tough one. We stare at problems beyond our control; circumstances spiral and attempt to pull us apart; evil appears to have the upper hand. Maybe the attack is personal, or maybe we recognize evil incidents taking place around us. We know we can't defeat it on our own, but "He who is in [us] is greater than he who is in the world" (1 John 4:4). God is all powerful, working on our behalf and in us by the Holy Spirit. May we know "the immeasurable greatness of His power toward us who believe, according to the working of His great might that He worked in Christ when He raised Him from the dead" (Ephesians 1:19–20).

The unseen reality of God's presence and power conquers any visible or hidden power of the enemy and those who do his bidding. Trust that your Savior, the One who holds the final victory on your behalf, is present and working in you today. Pray for eyes to see, hearts to trust, and minds to find assurance in His mighty strength.

All powerful is His love for us in Christ Jesus; nothing can separate us from it:

> We are more than conquerors through Him who loved us. For I am sure that neither death nor life, nor angels nor rulers, nor things present nor things to come, nor powers, nor height nor depth, nor anything else in all creation, will be able to separate us from the love of God in Christ Jesus our Lord. (Romans 8:37–39)

JOURNAL

During less-than-spectacular seasons, what has helped (or could help) you remember that God is still and always working? Write about a time when a slow season turned into a tough one. Choose one of the verses from this devotion to write and commit to memory to help you during these seasons.

PRAYER

Mighty God, You hold the final victory! Nothing can separate me from Your love in Christ . . .

WHY?

And we know that for those who love God all things work together for good, for those who are called according to His purpose. Romans 8:28

Countless nights I laid awake, wondering *why*. Like a lot of teens, I had questions about life and my place in it. *Why didn't guys give me a second glance? Why did I struggle with my self-image and my weight? Why did I have trouble finding friends?* I wondered if someone could see value in me when I struggled to see it in myself. One night I crawled out of bed and knelt on the floor, begging God through tears that, someday, a guy would truly love me, that friends would come my way too.

God taught me so much during those difficult teenage years. He developed patience in me as I learned to wait for answers that came much later. He worked through influential adults who spoke into my life regarding my value. In His timing, He showed me that He had much better relationships in store than the ones I prayed for on my knees that night. He heard my heart's cry.

Although we may see God's answers and provision at a later date, often we don't know the *why* during some of life's most difficult or challenging situations. That said, *we can always trust the who*. When we don't see an immediate response, it appears to us that He hasn't heard our cries—but it may be that He is working another way for a greater good, according to His wisdom and will. Maybe He is preventing something from falling into place the way we think it should. He knows what we need, even when we don't agree! His power may be revealed as He stops something, and not just when He brings something to pass.

There are countless ways God may use a difficult circumstance for your spiritual good. To name a few:

💜 He may lead you to look to your Savior for peace in tribulation.
   (John 16:33)

- He may teach you to rest in His strength and receive His help in times of trouble. (Psalm 46:1)

- He may grow and mature your faith in Him. (James 1:2–4)

Through trials and times of testing, remember that the *who* is God. He is working all things together for good—you have His Word on it. He may use a given situation to help you recognize your dependence on Him for peace, strength, and a growing faith. Trust God to work through every *why* for His purpose to which you are called in Christ! Maybe He will bring about changes in you, by His grace: from fearful to courageous, from anxious to peaceful, from wavering to steadfast in faith.

JOURNAL	PRAYER
Look up the referenced verses in today's devotion and personalize them to your specific situations. How do they speak to you or encourage you? How can knowing these things make a difference in your outlook in the coming week? month? year?	Lord God, though I often wonder why, I trust You to work all things together for good. Increase my faith . . .

CREATIVE AND
REDEMPTIVE POWER

His invisible attributes, namely, His eternal power and divine nature,
have been clearly perceived, ever since the creation of the world, in the
things that have been made. Romans 1:20

Since I'm a child of the Great Plains, my travels across the Big Island of Hawaii provided a new perspective. Eight of the earth's thirteen climate zones exist on this relatively tiny island. As my family and I left coastal Kona and drove inland, we encountered a tropical rainforest, then lush farmland, followed by rugged, rocky terrain in near-desert conditions. Later we visited an active volcano and learned that further inland were snow-capped mountain peaks.

Among the many fascinating things we learned was that cacao plants grow in almost every ecosystem on the island, and the varied climates and soil compositions produce distinct chocolate flavors. (These facts provided a great excuse to purchase products made from cacao grown in each environment!) This variety and specificity, found in something so simple as a chocolate-producing plant, is just one of countless examples of God's creative handiwork. Already in awe of His power in creation, I left the island with even greater wonder and a heart full of praise.

When we read Psalm 148, we join all of creation, praising the Lord for the work of His hands:

Let them praise the name of the Lord! For He commanded and they
were created. . . . Praise the Lord from the earth, you great sea crea-
tures and all deeps. . . . Mountains and all hills, fruit trees and all
cedars! Beasts and all livestock, creeping things and flying birds! Kings
of the earth and all peoples, princes and all rulers of the earth! Young
men and maidens together, old men and children! Let them praise the
name of the Lord. (Psalm 148:5, 9–13)

By the Lord's eternal power and divine nature (His invisible attributes, according to Romans 1:20), He spoke and the world came into being! He created "heaven and earth, and . . . all things visible and invisible," to quote the Nicene Creed. And His creative work continues today in every plant, every animal . . . every person. *You and I are uniquely made*, incomparably more distinct than Hawaii's cacao varieties—or any other creative masterpiece, for that matter. Praise the Lord!

With one glance, we should clearly perceive His creative power in all the "things that have been made." All of creation testifies to its Creator, but because of the fall, we fail. How often we forget to give Him glory and instead take it as our own. We suppress the truth; we fail to honor God or praise our Creator's name. Although we don't deserve it, by His redemptive power and out of His steadfast love, our Father sent His Son to save us, the pinnacle of His creation.

If anyone is in Christ, he is a new creation. The old has passed away; behold, the new has come. (2 Corinthians 5:17)

Chosen and redeemed by Christ, we are in fact a new creation. Praise the Lord!

JOURNAL

Read all of Psalm 148 and praise the Lord with the psalmist. Write about a particular piece of His creative work that you find fascinating. Look up and learn a few new facts about it.

PRAYER

Lord of all creation, I praise You for the infinite variety in Your handiwork . . . and for Your infinite power to create and redeem me . . .

POWER TO PROSPER

For as the rain and the snow come down from heaven and do not return there but water the earth, making it bring forth and sprout, giving seed to the sower and bread to the eater, so shall My word be that goes out from My mouth; it shall not return to Me empty, but it shall accomplish that which I purpose, and shall succeed in the thing for which I sent it. Isaiah 55:10–11

A winter walk across the pasture at my family's farm in South Dakota provides a familiar, but always breathtaking, view. As I walk, I gaze at chopped corn stalks peeking above a white blanket and snow-capped hills sprinkled with cedar trees. The cedars cluster closer in the low places where more moisture settles; there, the cattle take shelter in the winter.

Settled snow is always beautiful, but for the rancher, it means more work to complete daily chores. Nevertheless, heavy, wet snow soaks into the ground, runs into the creeks, and fills stock dams. While I gaze at the beauty of the snow over this land, my farm family understands it to be so much more. Rain and snow serve a great purpose: enabling grasses to grow, crops to sprout, and land to prosper. Someone who works the land understands firsthand the power of the connection provided by the Lord through the imagery in Isaiah's words above.

Today, as always, we can expect His Word to accomplish His purpose. *God's Word prospers everywhere* He sends it. He works powerfully through it, giving the good news of salvation and eternal life in Christ, instilling faith, transforming His people, and providing guidance.

God's desires and His plans are revealed to you in His Word. Even when you don't recognize the way it's speaking to you or how His plan will take shape, trust that He will work through His Word according to His purpose; it will not return to Him void. God's Word "shall succeed in the thing for which [He] sent it" . . . to you!

Ready for a good word from God? Sit at His feet, fold your hands in praise and prayer, and lean in to learn, no matter the amount of time you have, no matter the time of day, and no matter how you've failed or fallen short before. He meets you, forgives you, and embraces you; expect His powerful Word to work in and through you, accomplishing immeasurably more than you can imagine.

JOURNAL

As the Lord meets you in His Word, what is He telling you today? Open your Bible to a passage in the Gospel of John, then journal your thoughts and takeaways.

PRAYER

Holy Spirit, I praise You for Your power working through the Word. Guide me and fulfill Your plans through me . . .

CHILDLIKE WONDER

Show me the wonders of Your great love! Psalm 17:7, NIV

Is there anything quite like watching a child discover, see, or taste something wonderful for the first time? Which is the best part: the obvious delight, the captive attention, the twinkling eyes, or the gaping mouth? I have a friend who owns a chocolate shop. One festive day, the shop was giving away fresh samples, and a little boy came forward for one, already excited. *Free chocolate!* After popping it in his mouth, he froze. His eyes grew big, and he ran to his mom. "Mom, you gotta try one. It'll change your life!"

Watch a child delight in pure chocolate perfection . . . or the season's first snowfall . . . or the fur of a newborn puppy . . . all with wide eyes of wonder! Wonder. From it, we get the word *wonderful*—which we use more often. It means "full of wonder," but do we think of that when we proclaim something to be wonder-full?

We read of God's powerful signs and wonders done miraculously through Moses, the apostles, and others. Children of every age can't help but respond with wonder when we hear how our all-powerful God sent His Son, who was with God from the beginning, to redeem His people back to Himself.

Recall with renewed awe *the wonders of the love of God*, revealed in the fulfilled prophecies at Christ's birth, displayed across His creation (from the smallest cell to the expanse of the cosmos!), and demonstrated fully as He sent His Son to the cross in our place, the sacrifice that would pay for our sins, then restored Him to life and to His right hand.

David cries to the Lord in Psalm 17:7, "Show me the wonders of Your great love!" Was King David asking for greater revelation of the immeasurable love he already knew from the God he served? Or was he asking an all-powerful God to refresh the awe and wonder he'd once had?

The Creator, who formed you in His image, who fearfully and wonderfully made you (Psalm 139:14), says you are His workmanship—His masterpiece, created anew in Christ for the purposes He prepared in advance for you (Ephesians 2:10). May you and I embrace childlike wonder and proclaim of His powerful love, "It will change your life!"

JOURNAL

Do you find yourself in awestruck wonder of God's plan of salvation, fulfilled in the Savior? Journal what He has done for you. Ponder His power . . . then ask Him to refresh your wonder.

PRAYER

Dear Creator, give me childlike wonder as I delight in You . . .

POWER FOR THE WEAK

He said to me, "My grace is sufficient for you, for My power is made perfect in weakness." Therefore I will boast all the more gladly of my weaknesses, so that the power of Christ may rest upon me. For the sake of Christ, then, I am content with weaknesses, insults, hardships, persecutions, and calamities. For when I am weak, then I am strong. 2 Corinthians 12:9–10

This girl sadly lacks upper body strength. No matter the months of rigorous strength training or heavy lifting, I cannot lift my body weight with my arms. No chin-ups for me.

One summer, my husband and I braved a couples' fitness contest at our local YMCA. Our competitive spirits had us go the distance, sticking to the program director's weekly challenges, which included combinations of cardio and strength building. By the end of that summer, I was in the best shape of my adult life. Still: no chin-ups. Not. One. But my husband could do what I could not; where I was weak, he was strong. Thanks to our teamwork and our complementary strengths, we tasted victory. We took first place! (A first for me in any athletic endeavor.)

Others have been my strength (physical and spiritual) when I have lacked it myself. Incomparably more so, God provides the power I lack. I'm not afraid to say that weakness is my strong suit, and I admit I'm weak in ways that cannot compare to my puny upper arms. Far more significant is my weakness toward certain sins. I give in to gossip. I put my own desires ahead of others' needs. I fail to go the distance for my friends. I don't stick to things I've committed to, letting down others. I crumble when insults or calamities come my way.

I cry out, "Lord! This is just too hard for me," when I am lacking strength (which is every day, by the way). How do you and I trust His power and lean on Him? By His gifts of forgiveness and faith. The prophet Jeremiah proclaimed to the Lord, "Nothing is too hard for You!" (Jeremiah 32:17) as he recounted the mighty acts of God for His people. He did what we could not. In fact, He did all the heavy lifting on our behalf when He was lifted to the cross, dying in our place. *His strength* in us is the only way we taste sweet victory.

God's power was made even more evident in Paul's life as Paul recognized—and struggled in—his weakness. The power of Christ rested upon and worked through Paul. Because God's grace is sufficient, you and I can be content, as Paul was, with weaknesses and every other challenge or hardship we face. In Christ, "When [we] are weak, [we] are strong" (2 Corinthians 12:10).

As for this weak woman, I'll never be able to complete a single chin-up. But I can keep my chin up because victory is mine in Christ, thanks be to God! His power rests upon me.

JOURNAL

In what ways do you most recognize your weakness? Spiritually speaking, what personal strength training will you engage in today, allowing God to work in you? Who could partner with you to help you stick to it?

PRAYER

Lord Jesus, Your power rests upon me. Give me contentment, by Your grace . . .

HORIZONS

For we know in part and we prophesy in part, but when the perfect comes, the partial will pass away. . . . For now we see in a mirror dimly, but then face to face. Now I know in part; then I shall know fully, even as I have been fully known. 1 Corinthians 13:9–10, 12

I looked toward the horizon at what appeared to be an endless ocean. With no sight of land, I was struck with the thought of how limited my view was from my current vantage point, even though I could see an incalculable distance of sea. I could circle the ship and still see only water. I gazed out at a deep blue hue, with the occasional wisp of white atop a small wave, and a distinct line where the ocean met the sky.

The horizon line isn't really a line at all, but merely the limit or extent of our present perspective, our current view. Our limited view doesn't mean that's all there is or that what's beyond our current view will be the same as what we see now. Tomorrow's vantage point will be different, and, there-fore, so will the picture of what we see. We can't possibly know all. But God can . . . and does. His view is infinite. His power is infinite too.

In His wisdom and by His grace, the Lord doesn't allow us to see clearly beyond today's view; it would be more than we could comprehend or handle in this life. He has provided all we need in order to *hold onto hope* for tomorrow through His prophecies and promises, by His Word. Only God is privy to the full landscape beyond today's view. But "when the perfect comes" in the day of Christ's return, we will know fully too. Until then, we have the amazing opportunity to trust the only One who does.

There is no limit to God's vision; no horizon line for Him. And with each new day and each horizon we face, He offers His wisdom and grace by faith in Christ. Since He knows the landscape, the view, and our paths beyond our current horizon, we can trust Him with each new day and receive what we need, right now, from His Word, a lamp for our feet and a light for our paths (Psalm 119:105). We can trust Him to do far more abundantly than all we ask or think, according to His all-knowing power at work within us and in the world.

When the tough questions come our way, like "What's the next right thing to do?" "How can I respond to this person?" or "Where should I place my priorities?" may our first thought lead us to another question: "What does God's Word say?" With His perfect vision, He leads our way toward the next horizon . . . and the next.

JOURNAL

From today's limited perspective, write about your current view. What question do you have for God today? How does it help to know that His view is limitless?

PRAYER

Lord God, I have all that I need in You. Help me trust You with every new view . . .

ENCOURAGING WORDS

Therefore encourage one another and build one another up, just as you are doing. 1 Thessalonians 5:11

After my sister, Connie, and I arrived at the airport for the national convention for Lutheran Women in Mission, we stood outside the terminal for three hours, waiting for the hotel shuttle. Because a few thousand people were arriving for this convention on the same day, I was not surprised to find a dear friend from another part of the country waiting for the same shuttle.

As my friend and I took this unexpected opportunity to catch up, I introduced her to Connie, and she introduced both of us to the pastor traveling with her group. One topic led to another, and soon the pastor and Connie learned they shared a similar circumstance: they each have a child with the same medical diagnosis. While my sister's son has lived with the disease for many years, the pastor's son had been diagnosed only months earlier. He expressed his family's fears; Connie provided perspective and peace. He asked questions; she humbly offered what she'd learned through years of experience and research. He shared his family's hesitation to try a new device; with compassion, she reasoned with him to give it a try. Soon after, the conversation ended when we boarded our shuttle.

Nearly a year later, a speaking opportunity took me to that same friend's part of the country, and this pastor approached me. He had a tearful message he wanted me to share with my sister: "She changed our lives." *What?!* Words tumbled from this dear man as he told how he was moved by Connie's encouragement, advice, and compelling argument to "give it a try." He had called his wife from the convention that evening to say, "I think we need to do this." It was a game-changer for the health and future of their son and, therefore, for their family. He gave all the glory to God, but he also conveyed a hearty thanks to Connie.

I called Connie and relayed the pastor's message to her. She was shocked and humbled by his kind and generous words. It was her turn for tears as she thanked God for His power at work through her as He used her supportive words to make a big difference for this family. The Lord accomplished immeasurably more through Connie's advice and encouraging words than any of us could have imagined!

The Lord is compassionate and merciful (James 5:11), and because He works powerfully in us by the Holy Spirit, we can be conduits of His mercy. Chosen and covered in Christ by His forgiveness, we can "put on . . . compassionate hearts, kindness, humility, meekness, and patience" (Colossians 3:12).

Where may you be called to speak kind and compassionate words? Trust God to provide through you as you humbly respond to others in helpful ways and as God has accordingly equipped you with wisdom through similar experience. We serve a mighty God as we serve His people.

JOURNAL

Write about an opportunity you've been given to be a conduit of God's mercy. How has God provided through you to someone in need?

PRAYER

Dear Lord God, show me where I can be helpful today. Work in me, by the Spirit's power . . .

IMMEASURABLY MORE
Provision

JESUS MATH

Now when it was evening, the disciples came to [Jesus] and said, "This is a desolate place, and the day is now over; send the crowds away to go into the villages and buy food for themselves." But Jesus said, "They need not go away; you give them something to eat." They said to Him, "We have only five loaves here and two fish." And He said, "Bring them here to Me." Then He ordered the crowds to sit down on the grass, and taking the five loaves and the two fish, He looked up to heaven and said a blessing. Then He broke the loaves and gave them to the disciples, and the disciples gave them to the crowds. And they all ate and were satisfied. And they took up twelve baskets full of the broken pieces left over. And those who ate were about five thousand men, besides women and children. Matthew 14:15–21

Do we look at a lack of supply the same way the disciples did? With defeat? They added the issues: (1) it was late; (2) no one lived in that desolate place; (3) there was no way they could afford (time or cost) to feed this multitude. The disciples decided, based on evidence, that Jesus should send everyone away. In John's account of this event, we learn that Philip had even done the math: "Two hundred denarii worth of bread would not be enough for each of them to get a little" (John 6:7). Feeding the people didn't add up!

Jesus did more than anyone could have imagined, and He did it through His doubting disciples. "You give them something to eat" (Matthew 14:16). He took a simple lunch that wasn't meant to feed more than one or two, gave thanks to the Father for it, and set His disciples to work. Jesus' miraculous provision came through them; He broke the bread, handed it to them, and they distributed it to five thousand men, plus women and children.

In perfect trust, Jesus gave thanks to the Father before the miracle occurred. Our Savior turned one meal into such abundance that the leftovers alone would have fed a small village. And perhaps they did!

When we add up an issue or calculate a problem, do we factor in Jesus? What simple lunch do you have that the Lord may choose to use for immeasurably more? Show up. Release your basket into the hands of the One who will hold it before the Father, then dole it out in generous provision for others. When you do, is there any less for you? As recorded in Luke 6, Jesus said, "Give, and it will be given to you. Good measure, pressed down, shaken together, running over, will be put into your lap. For with the measure you use it will be measured back to you" (v. 38).

I've done the math when our means were few. And I don't say this tritely: *God provided. Every. Time.* When we can't see the *how* in the moment, we always know the *who*, even as He uses His people to distribute our provision, much as He handed the bread to His disciples.

Take your problem, need, or depletion to Jesus. Trust Him to work miraculously through you or through someone He sends your way. Don't underestimate the abundant measure of His provision or the miraculous math Jesus can do.

JOURNAL

Make a list of tangible or practical ways you help others. Then imagine how Jesus may increase your service, even exponentially, by His miraculous provision, whether you know it or not.

PRAYER

Jesus, lead me to release my circumstances to You . . . use them as You will . . .

RICH PROVISION

As for the rich in this present age, charge them not to be haughty, nor to set their hopes on the uncertainty of riches, but on God, who richly provides us with everything to enjoy. They are to do good, to be rich in good works, to be generous and ready to share. 1 Timothy 6:17–18

I visited a friend in her nicer-than-mine home, and I was truly happy for her, commenting on the rooms' unique designs, appreciating her eye for detail, and telling her how much I enjoyed our time together. Then, en route home, envy grabbed hold of me; it had snuck through a door I didn't realize I'd opened for it. Without warning, I found myself wishing I could afford her home and her things. Then I began guilting myself over my life and career choices, certain these were the reasons I couldn't afford what I envied. And the snowball kept rolling . . . pretty soon I was wondering about life, my value, and my priorities.

With God's help, I can stop the snowball effect and say, "Wait a minute!" Greater means would not necessarily bring all the niceties I had wrapped my thoughts around. Maybe we could have more; maybe not. Maybe if we had greater wealth, God would lead us to use it in a different way.

Truth be told, I am among "the rich in this present age," and while I know I should not set my hope on the uncertainty of riches, sometimes I invite envy in. The apostle Paul warns, "Let us not become conceited . . . envying one another" (Galatians 5:26). Convicted, I confess my misplaced hope, *confident of God's forgiveness for me in Christ*.

I remember the ways God has richly provided for my family and me, time and again. He created me with value and has given me passion for the work I do. I want to "do good, to be rich in good works, to be generous and ready to share." And He will do far more than I'll ever know, by His power at work in me.

By God's grace, may you and I remember His provision and our priorities in Christ when envy is at the door and wanting a welcome. May we count our blessings, quite literally. And may we be truly glad for our friends, celebrating with them in God's provision for their lives too, remembering that every good gift is ultimately from Him (James 1:17).

JOURNAL

Start listing blessings and count them . . . and keep adding each day. (With gratitude for God's provision, you can keep envy outside.) Then begin a list of ways you can share generously out of God's rich supply to you.

PRAYER

Heavenly Father, please forgive me for inviting envy in. Thank You for Your rich provision in Christ . . .

WAITING FOR A SIGN

Now Jesus did many other signs in the presence of the disciples, which are not written in this book; but these are written so that you may believe that Jesus is the Christ, the Son of God, and that by believing you may have life in His name. John 20:30–31

On the coffee shop's counter was a sign that simply said: "Are you waiting for a sign? THIS IS IT." I burst out laughing, snapped a photo, and then started thinking. *What kind of sign have I been waiting for of late?* Maybe, just maybe, this silly sign was it.

"What should I do, Lord?" I ask. Sometimes I'm so busy waiting or watching for some kind of sign from Him that I don't seize opportunities that come my way:

- That person I "accidentally" ran into at the store, from whom I received much-needed encouragement.
- The invitation for coffee and prayer together that followed.
- This unexpected opportunity to serve.
- The good news from God that I received when I read His Word!

For centuries, God's people heard the prophets' words and watched for signs, waiting for the promised Savior. On the night of Jesus' birth, an angel told shepherds in a nearby field how to find the newborn King:

This will be a sign for you: you will find a baby wrapped in swaddling cloths and lying in a manger. (Luke 2:12)

Later, Wise Men received a sign: a star in the night sky that led them to the infant King (Matthew 2).

Just after Jesus miraculously fed over five thousand people with two fish and five loaves of bread, the crowds craned their necks even closer, demanding more signs and miracles:

Then what sign do you do, that we may see and believe you? What work do you perform? (John 6:30)

But they were missing the mark. More than a mere sign, the Savior Himself— the fulfillment of every divine sign—was right in front of them! The One who fed them bread, performing this miraculous sign and so many others, was the very bread of life. Jesus said:

For the bread of God is He who comes down from heaven and gives life to the world. . . . I am the bread of life; whoever comes to Me shall not hunger, and whoever believes in Me shall never thirst. . . . Truly, truly, I say to you, who- ever believes has eternal life. I am the bread of life. (John 26:33, 35, 47–48)

We can only imagine the number of signs Jesus provided throughout His ministry, revealing Himself to be God the Son and the promised Savior. Recorded in the Gospels are just a portion of His signs, but by the work of the Spirit, these were *written so that we may believe!*

God speaks to us in His Word, and as He reveals His work by the power of the Spirit working through us into one another's lives, we can remember the *sign* of the cross placed upon us in our Baptism, marking each of us as one who is redeemed in Christ by faith. Saved from our sin, we have life in His name. And we're called according to His purpose (Romans 8:28). This is our sign!

JOURNAL

At the heart of God's provision is a Savior. Name opportunities that have come your way of late, all signs of His provision through His Word and through you to others.

PRAYER

Lord, I praise You for every sign You've provided, pointing me to Christ!

A THRILL OF HOPE

For the grace of God has appeared, bringing salvation for all people
. . . [as we wait] for our blessed hope, the appearing of the glory of
our great God and Savior Jesus Christ, who gave Himself for us
to redeem us. Titus 2:11, 13–14

There is one Christmas song I sing all year long! Whether it's May or December, if you're nearby, you'll hear me singing "O holy night! the stars are brightly shining; It is the night of the dear Savior's birth." A few phrases send a chill, and especially this one: "A thrill of hope, the weary world rejoices!" A thrill. It's THRILLING!

We usually reserve thrilling for rare, exhilarating moments, all gifts from God:

The breathtaking view atop a mountain after making the climb.

The moment we receive the promotion, the award, the good news.

The surprise of a long-distance loved one who suddenly appears at the door.

Those moments are thrilling! They produce a wave of emotion, but more than that—a recognition that we've witnessed or received something wonderful or beautiful. Thrilling moments can be fleeting and far between. But what about a thrill . . . of hope?

"Long lay the world in sin and error pining, 'Til He appeared and the soul felt its worth." Do you know the measure of your worth in the Father's eyes? You are worth the price of His Son, paid to redeem your soul from sin, death, and the power of the devil.

When He appeared at the cross, bloodied and crucified . . . to redeem us.

When He appeared before the women at the empty tomb and to the disciples—risen and victorious!

When He appears in glory on the Last Day, when He raises us up and takes us home to Him for eternity.

Is there anything more thrilling than this good news? A thrill of hope rises in our hearts because we know that in Christ, the guilt of our sin is gone! In Christ, our hope is sure and certain. God handed us hope in the manger, and He secured our hope at the cross and the empty tomb. In God's perfect provision, we have the hope of salvation—eternal life in Christ.

This hope impacts every part of our lives. It assures us of our identity in Him; it gives us purpose and enables us to proclaim God's Good News to a weary world full of dying people who have no hope because they don't yet know they have a Savior.

So go ahead, let a thrill of hope wash over you!

"Rejoice in hope" (Romans 12:12). Jesus is at work in your life now, filling you with hope. Better than the most breathtaking view of God's creation and greater than any other milestone moment or sudden surprise, we receive a thrill of hope—not fleeting or far-between, but now and forever, enduring and eternal. (Thrilling, isn't it?)

JOURNAL

Describe a few thrilling moments and memories. What stands out to you from today's devotion regarding your hope in Christ? His resurrection? His return? His Good News that's yours to share?

PRAYER

God of grace, I thrill in the hope I have in Jesus!

SQUIRREL!

Blessed is the man who makes the L<small>ORD</small> his trust, who does not turn to the proud, to those who go astray after a lie! You have multiplied, O L<small>ORD</small> my God, Your wondrous deeds and Your thoughts toward us; none can compare with You! I will proclaim and tell of them, yet they are more than can be told. Psalm 40:4–5

As my friend Debbie and I shared in ministry travels, we realized we had more in common than our name and our love for Jesus. Both chatterboxes, we shared a flight without one moment of silence between us, bouncing from one topic to another. Pretty soon, we'd wandered . . . again . . . and started shouting *"Squirrel!"* to each other, in turn. We even purchased felted wool squirrels at the airport as reminders of our shared travel adventure and our similar tendencies to *"Squirrel!"* amid any topic of conversation.

So many topics vie for our attention on any given day, and in our tech-obsessed world, there is no shortage of sources for distraction. Scrolling through social media for an edifying message, we catch glimpses of others' highlight reels or filtered photos, and suddenly we've forgotten our initial focus. We view countless ads promising financial security, prolonged beauty, or certain success (if we opt in). We receive tempting offers for weight loss (following four major payments) or happiness (in three easy steps). It's no wonder people are distracted at every turn and dissatisfied with the status quo as they attempt to go about their lives. *"Squirrel!" "What? Where?"* When could we, too, be tempted to "go astray after a lie," according to the psalmist?

Social media has some merit when posts lead us to the Word, point us to Christ, or teach us something of value that lines up with Scripture, but how often, in our admitted distraction—*"Squirrel!"*—do we end up viewing something that leads our minds to wander away from truth? When may we mistakenly place our trust in something other than the Lord alone?

There is only one place we will find eternal security, true beauty, and victory for today and forever (which is better than success by some worldly standard). What is this place? *God's pure and perfect Word.* The world can't offer what the Word does: peace by faith in Christ Jesus and the assurance of salvation in Him alone.

For all the messages vying for our attention, may we return to the one of greatest value, beyond compare: Jesus' saving love. By His grace, He forgives us when we've chased after squirrels of every kind. By His power, we can "[fix] our eyes on Jesus, the pioneer and perfecter of faith" (Hebrews 12:2, NIV). We make the Lord our trust. His provision is immeasurable; His "wondrous deeds and [His] thoughts toward us" are innumerable. As we join the psalmist, proclaiming and telling of them, we trust that God will be glorified!

JOURNAL

In a world saturated with distractions, what will help you focus on Christ and His incomparable message for you? What ways can you proclaim and tell of them? Face to face? Via social media?

PRAYER

Lord, "turn my eyes from looking at worthless things; and give me life in Your ways" (Psalm 119:37) . . .

YOUR WORK MATTERS

For it is God who works in you, both to will and to work for His good pleasure. Philippians 2:13

What's on your schedule today? Will you work in the office or from home? Are you studying because the next test is tomorrow? Will you work with your hands, crunching numbers or creating new products? Are you interacting with a team or operating alone? What skills will you use? What gifts do you employ for the benefit of your family and others?

That's a long list of questions, and maybe your answers vary depending on the day. The point to my plethora of questions is one more question:

Do you believe your work makes a difference?

Oh sure, it may provide a portion or all of your income, but did you know that God does immeasurably more in and through your work than you realize? The task you completed on behalf of your team meant more to someone behind the scenes than you will ever know. The endless hours of menial labor for your family speak volumes to growing children who watch your every move and will emulate them in the future. The skills you offer in the classroom, at church, or in your community will be used to impact someone—or many—for good, and God is glorified through you.

Your work matters. It matters to those who benefit from it, both directly and indirectly, and it matters to God. Ultimately, it is God working in and through you by the *Holy Spirit's power* (and isn't that exciting?!). He provides you with the desire and with the ability to accomplish work that is pleasing to Him (Philippians 2:13) and for His purpose. He is glorified when you work with "sincerity of heart, fearing the Lord" (Colossians 3:22). Remember that as you "work heartily, as for the Lord and not for men . . . you are serving the Lord Christ" (vv. 23–24).

A watching world takes notice. So, what can you do when your heart is just not in your work? Pray. Confess your struggle or shortcomings to the

One who freely forgives you in Christ. Then, with a repentant heart, act. With His help, you can give it all you've got as you ask Him to help your heart catch up. You have the privilege of serving the Lord Christ when you serve others.

Just as God provides all you need in order to accomplish the work He has for you, He also provides for others through you. When you work to the glory of God, you imitate Christ. (Amazing, right?) Jesus said,

My Father is working until now, and I am working. (John 5:17)

Our times—including every working hour—are in His hand.

JOURNAL	PRAYER
God provides in a plethora of ways, and He chooses to do it through you! Write why you believe your work matters and who benefits from it. How do you recognize God's provision through you to others?	Dear God, work in me daily for Your good pleasure. I can give it all I've got because I've got You . . .

ANSWERED PRAYER

[Jesus said,] "Whatever you ask in My name, this I will do, that the Father may be glorified in the Son. If you ask Me anything in My name, I will do it." John 14:13–14

My dear friend Lois pauses during her personal Bible study time when someone comes to mind as she reads. She stops to pray. Many days, I've been the recipient of her prayers. On one such day, Lois reached out to me after her prayer on my behalf. She texted her concerns and prayers for me, which spoke specifically to my needs, though I had expressed them only to God. He heard my cries, and He answered Lois's prayer, lifted out of concern for me. That day, I was encouraged and emboldened in my faith; I'd received a reminder of His intimate care and miraculous provision through prayer. May I always be so quick to give Him glory as I did that day!

While God continuously provides for us, how often do we take notice? I mean really take notice? When are you most alert to His specific care? Do you recognize when His provision comes in direct answer to prayer? I wonder how many miracles you and I have missed because we weren't waiting for an answer or watching in expectation for Him to act. Maybe we missed it because it came from an unexpected direction. I admit, I am often oblivious or quick to assume that a resultant action or answer to prayer is coincidence. *Ouch!*

God's active response to our prayers should not surprise us. Instead, may it excite us, fill us with awe, and lead us to praise our almighty provider, giving glory to the Father in His Son, our Savior!

Did you know that your humble prayer lifted to the Father in Jesus' name will accomplish immeasurably more than you ask, according to His purpose? *His hand is upon you*, your surroundings, and your situations. Look for His fingerprints as He acts according to His Word.

Pray for one another, that you may be healed. The prayer of a righteous person has great power as it is working. (James 5:16)

When I watch expectantly as I pray, I am more likely to recognize God's answer and His care.

Continue steadfastly in prayer, being watchful in it with thanksgiving. (Colossians 4:2)

I won't always see His response, but when I do, I grow in trust, time and again, thanks be to God! As I grow in Him, I notice my desires change to reflect His will, His plans, and His purpose for me. The desires of His heart become mine, and I pray for them in Jesus' name.

Delight yourself in the LORD, and He will give you the desires of your heart. (Psalm 37:4)

By God's grace, my heart aligns with His will as I delight in the Lord.

JOURNAL

Write about one of the countless times God answered your prayers. Start (or continue) a practice of recording your prayer requests in your journal. When you read through past requests, you'll be more likely to recognize answers as evidence of God's work.

PRAYER

Dear Lord God, embolden me in my prayers for others, trusting that You will answer according to Your purpose and will, as I pray in Jesus' name . . .

MIRACULOUS SUPPLY

And God is able to make all grace abound to you, so that having all sufficiency in all things at all times, you may abound in every good work. As it is written, "He has distributed freely, He has given to the poor; His righteousness endures forever." He who supplies seed to the sower and bread for food will supply and multiply your seed for sowing and increase the harvest of your righteousness. 2 Corinthians 9:8–10

The oil was nearly gone. Then what? How would this widow feed her family? Because of her debt, she faced creditors coming for her boys, her only possession, as payment for this debt. She turned to God by turning to His prophet Elisha. The woman admitted what little she had to offer: a bit of oil. Following Elisha's instruction, she gathered empty jars from her neighbors. God would use the little oil she had to provide immeasurably, miraculously more! She poured from her meager supply, and the oil continued flowing until all the jars she had collected were full. As soon as she filled the last jar, the oil stopped flowing. God's provision was perfect. *Complete.* With her multiplied supply, she paid her debt in full (2 Kings 4:1–7).

Our needs, entrusted to God, are His opportunity to supply generously for us. "And my God will supply every need of yours according to His riches in glory in Christ Jesus" (Philippians 4:19). Think of those ordinary, empty jars, worth so little that neighbors gave them away. God uses ordinary vessels and fills them for His purpose. He not only supplies, He multiplies miraculously! And His provision is perfect; it may not always come in ways we want, but it will always arrive in ways we need.

Similarly, we are ordinary, earthen vessels. However, God willed that we would not be purchased to pay our own debt of sin; He would send His Son in our place to cover our debt in full. Jesus paid the price; we receive the credit. By God's miraculous outpouring, we are filled with faith, by the Holy Spirit. What's more, we now, by faith, contain the treasure of the Gospel (2 Corinthians 4:7).

The widow had little to offer the Lord. We have nothing to offer an almighty God in exchange for His grace, but we receive it in overflowing measure. He distributes freely! And get this: all of God's grace abounds (overflows!) to you → so you have all sufficiency → in all things → at all times → you may abound in every good work!

Maybe you start with just a little seed for sowing the Gospel. Trust Him to multiply your seed miraculously; you can expect a huge harvest.

JOURNAL

What good work has God called you to? With what gifts has He supplied you, that He may use . . . and multiply for His purpose? Your talents? A little bit of oil or one little seed?

PRAYER

Lord, Your grace overflows to me! May I overflow in every good work . . .

GIVING AND RECEIVING

Blessed be the God and Father of our Lord Jesus Christ, the Father of mercies and God of all comfort, who comforts us in all our affliction, so that we may be able to comfort those who are in any affliction, with the comfort with which we ourselves are comforted by God. For as we share abundantly in Christ's sufferings, so through Christ we share abundantly in comfort too. 2 Corinthians 1:3–5

My friend was accustomed to giving. When she learned that another family in her church or neighborhood was facing a crisis or in need of help, she and her family were some of the first to step forward. She found joy in running errands, providing meals, offering child care . . . and all with a listening ear when that was needed too. Then a crisis hit my friend's home, and she admitted to me how humbling and hard it was to graciously receive the kind of help that had been so easy to give. She learned, over time, to receive well, especially when she recognized the joy her friends and neighbors received in giving.

While we don't give so we can receive, let's practice both with grace and humility. After all, every good and perfect gift is ultimately from the hand of God (James 1:17), and none of us can outgive Him! *He is the supplier* of every need—tangible, spiritual, and eternal. And often, He provides for us through one another.

My family has been blessed and humbled, time and again, through the generous gifts of others. We have received everything from meals to hand-me-downs to financial support and more. And we've welcomed less-tangible gifts of time, godly counsel, and comfort—invaluable gifts, to be sure.

As God uses others to extend His comfort, may we live with open, extended hands.

My former mentor and fellow pastor's wife whom my friends and I affectionately called "Mother Marian" told me several times, "Give 'em a soft place to land, Deb." Sometimes, she was talking about my husband and the comfort God provides him through me. Other times, she expressed this sentiment more broadly, recognizing our own reception of God's grace and comfort in affliction and our opportunity to share what God first gave us: a soft place to land. God gives us grace in abundance in Jesus Christ (Romans 5:17). As we rest in the comfort of His embrace, we can be an instrument of His grace to others.

Our Savior provides at just the right time. He sends resources through the hands of others when they're most needed. He provides courage today to cope with today's fear. He will give wisdom tomorrow for tomorrow's decision. And what do we need, beyond all else? JESUS. In Him, we truly have all we need because God has richly supplied us with a Savior. He gives and we receive. Amen.

JOURNAL

Write about a time you were the blessed recipient of someone's care, gifts, or comfort. How did it feel to receive? Who is God leading you to help, that you may provide a soft place for someone to land?

PRAYER

Lord, I am humbled by Your provision through others, but most of all, by Your provision of Jesus . . .

BETTER TOGETHER

And let us consider how to stir up one another to love and good works, not neglecting to meet together, as is the habit of some, but encouraging one another, and all the more as you see the Day drawing near. Hebrews 10:24–25

Following a crisis in our community, a few women in my church reached out to me individually to express a need for one another's support and care. Word spread, and more women wondered how we could come together to support those who were hurting, encourage one another regularly, and love one another well. After all, the Lord exhorts us to "love one another with brotherly affection. Outdo one another in showing honor" (Romans 12:10).

Where could we create a space for women to meet, honor each other's needs, gather in the Word, and connect with one another? Crisis caused us to see, more than before, that we needed one another. We adopted the phrase "better together" and a new women's ministry began: Women's Connect.

In [Christ] you also are being built together into a dwelling place for God by the Spirit. (Ephesians 2:22)

As Paul spoke to the believers in Ephesus, he was telling them they were united in Christ, both Jews and Gentiles, brought together by a shared faith in Him and filled with the same Spirit! The Lord tells us by the same Word today that we, too, are being *built together*, the same Spirit living in each of us.

Through Women's Connect, all can come together. Some have followed Jesus since Baptism; others are new to the faith. Some arrive hungry to receive; others are ready to give. All come together with different backgrounds, experiences, and struggles. All need Jesus . . . and one another. When one is hurting, where will she turn? When another needs forgiveness, who will point her to Christ? When someone needs prayer, how will she seek support? (See James 5:16.) When still another has good news to share, who will she contact? The Lord exhorts us through Paul's words in Romans 12:15 to "rejoice with those who rejoice, weep with those who weep." He uses crises, difficulties, and even tragedy to bring His people together, and He works powerfully through each of us. We stir up one another to show love and to do good works, as iron sharpens iron (Proverbs 27:17).

Still today, God does immeasurably more through these women than any of them can ask or imagine, according to the Spirit, who dwells in each of them. We are better together as we meet together, united in Christ, "together . . . with one voice glorify[ing] the God and Father of our Lord Jesus Christ" (Romans 15:6).

JOURNAL

Write about some of your "better together" connections. Consider who you can connect with this week, to stir up and encourage. What might that look like?

PRAYER

Dear God, thank You for building believers together in Christ, filling us with the same Spirit . . .

IMMEASURABLY MORE
Purpose

MORE: FOR GOD'S GLORY

Do nothing from selfish ambition or conceit, but in humility count others more significant than yourselves. Philippians 2:3

As followers of Jesus, we are called according to God's purpose (Romans 8:28). *God's purpose!* Did you catch that? Amazing! As you and I consider His purpose . . . alongside His ability to do immeasurably more through it, let's ask one another, "Who benefits with *more*?" You? Me? What if, instead, *more* looks like upholding, helping, or supporting someone else? Sounds simple, right? But let's say that in order to uphold or help someone, we must surrender our agenda—our grand ambition for *more* as recognizable to us.

Our culture might try to twist our purpose and the pursuit of immeasurably more into a pursuit that is centered on self-indulgence, self-help, and self-celebration. We want more stuff, more attention, and more accolades. Only by *God's grace for us in Christ* can we humbly turn these ambitions around so they're aimed at others. According to God's purpose, let's provide someone else with a real pick-me-up by extending His lavish love to her. Let's open our arms to a homebound neighbor, honoring him with our time and our listening ear. Let's celebrate a loved one's accomplishment or milestone event by giving glory to God while rejoicing alongside her.

What does *immeasurably more* look like when *others* includes someone you struggle with? Jesus said,

But if anyone slaps you on the right cheek, turn to him the other also. And if anyone would sue you and take your tunic, let him have your cloak as well. And if anyone forces you to go one mile, go with him two miles. (Matthew 5:39–41)

Turn the other cheek and go the extra mile for someone who has hurt you; "love your enemies and pray for those who persecute you" (v. 44).

How is this even possible? Only as we walk in God's grace and serve according to the strength He provides can we take one humble step in someone's direction. Isn't it amazing that the Lord chooses to work through us at all? But He does.

We may also ask if God would be glorified through our actions, motives, and the purpose for which we work, serve, go, and do.

God is glorified as we love others well. And we can expect Him to do immeasurably more through our humble actions toward them. We may never know the extent of our impact, but God's purpose prevails, and He is glorified . . . and that's what matters most.

JOURNAL

What do you think surrender looks like regarding your agenda or grand ambitions for *more*? Brainstorm some ideas for upholding, supporting, or celebrating someone else to the glory of God.

PRAYER

Dear God, please forgive me for my selfish ambition. Give me a humble heart aimed toward others . . .

WHAT ARE YOU PRODUCING?

But the fruit of the Spirit is love, joy, peace, patience, kindness, goodness, faithfulness, gentleness, self-control. Galatians 5:22–23

In a world of accomplishments where people proudly sport badges of busyness, I have panicked, certain that I am not doing enough good, accomplishing my potential, or producing enough stuff. I end up rating my day based on what I've achieved or the tasks I've checked off.

I have itemized lists and detailed calendars, and I know that both help me stay on task, increase efficiency, and provide a visual reminder that holds me accountable. However, I've given so much emphasis to the task at hand, along with my desire to check things off my list, that I've failed to look up. In my doing, do I miss the bigger picture? Do I look up to see the *why* behind the *what* that I do?

God is much more interested in my *continued transformation* (Romans 12:2) and my love for others that results from it (1 John 4:19) than in how I've busied myself or what I've produced. Far more significant is the Holy Spirit's transformative work in me and who I am becoming in Christ so that the world may see Him through me. His power at work in me changes my heart. I'm a work in progress for sure, but I am ever growing toward having a heart more like Jesus', conforming to His image (Romans 8:29), and loving like He does. And so are you.

As we work, raise families, volunteer, and use our skill sets, are we able to practice patience? Treat others with kindness? Show self-control? Produce other fruits too? Yes! By God's grace for us, the Holy Spirit produces these fruits and more (Galatians 5:22–23). The Holy Spirit is also working through the fruit He produces, and not just in the tasks themselves. Relationships outweigh efficiency and productivity every day, and they teach us much about why we make a to-do list in the first place.

On my own, my accomplishments will come up short, but God's promised work in me and through me won't. At the end of the (every) day, it's not about my personal productivity; it's about His promise to do immeasurably more than I can imagine, through His Spirit-produced fruit. If I must sport a badge, may it be covered with fruit and point others to Christ.

JOURNAL

When might your to-do list take precedence over people? Write about your *why* behind the *what* that you do. List the Holy Spirit's fruits from Galatians 5 (above), and prayerfully consider an application for each one.

PRAYER

Dear Jesus, continue Your transforming work in me, by the Spirit . . .

VESSEL

Do you not know that your body is a temple of the Holy Spirit within you, whom you have from God? You are not your own, for you were bought with a price. So glorify God in your body. 1 Corinthians 6:19–20

"Will I have any self-control at tonight's buffet?" "I'm afraid to step on the scale." "I hate how I look in my clothes." Food anxiety. Body insecurity. Have either of these issues gripped you? Maybe not, but it's likely that you've questioned your outward appearance in some manner. Worldly value is given to a woman who achieves or maintains a perfect body, according to some unattainable, even unhealthy, standard. This so-called perfection doesn't exist, but I've fallen for the fallacy that it does. And when I did, I believed lies about my image, identity, and purpose, and I told myself stories that don't match what God tells me.

What lies have you believed about yourself that could make you forget your purpose? Giving someone or something the power to make you anxious or insecure can lead you to overlook your true purpose, for which God created you brand-new in Christ:

For we are His workmanship, created in Christ Jesus for good works, which God prepared beforehand, that we should walk in them. (Ephesians 2:10)

With the help of God and those He has placed near me, I've been able to identify these lies and throw them out, replacing them with *God's truth* and filling myself with it. I have learned that my body is a vessel, created and fashioned by God for His purpose. It's a temple that houses the Holy Spirit! May I see my body as an offering to the Lord, a living sacrifice (Romans 12:1), in service to Him as I serve others. I am not my own, praise the Lord! Rather, I belong to Him, purchased at the price of Jesus' sacrifice for me.

May you and I celebrate our physical attributes and our bodily image because these vessels, though weak, contain the treasure of the Gospel:

But we have this treasure in jars of clay, to show that the surpassing power belongs to God and not to us. (2 Corinthians 4:7)

Our bodies enable us to truly be Jesus' hands and feet; they lead us to our neighbor. Our arms readily embrace. Our eyes see where there is need. Our mouths speak grace and truth, proclaiming the Gospel of Christ as we live by faith in Him. If our bodies are limited in mobility, may those limitations merely remind us that we rely on Jesus, who does immeasurably more than we can even ask, and He chooses to work through us by the Spirit! He may choose to connect us with others who have similar needs or those who can meet our needs by way of their hands and feet.

I want to be purposeful with my body, eager to serve and not stopped by insecurity or shamed by my physical shortcomings. May I love the body God gave me and give Him the glory. After all, the surpassing power within me belongs to Him who does immeasurably more!

JOURNAL

What lies have you believed concerning your body? How can you honor God with your body? What may serve as a daily reminder that your body is a temple? Choose one of the verses in this devotion to commit to memory.

PRAYER

Lord God, thank You for giving me this body; I am fearfully and wonderfully made! Show me how and where I can live out my purpose today . . .

RIPPLE EFFECT

The grace of our Lord overflowed for me with the faith and love that are in Christ Jesus. 1 Timothy 1:14

When someone creates a splash—think "Cannonball!"—water spatters, sprays, and surges in all directions. If you're nearby, you may get drenched. If you're a bit farther away, you may or may not get splashed, but you will feel the ripple effect. Even further away, the ripple ring may not be as deep, but it will be wider.

What's the difference between the ripple effect of a literal water splash and the ripple effect that happens when the Lord makes a splash through us? Water ripples grow slighter with distance, and though the rings grow wider, they eventually diminish. The ripple effect of our witness for Christ has the potential to grow both wider and deeper as it increases exponentially, carried forward by others whose own splashes create new ripples. The effect never ends.

What could that look like in your corner of the world? "Out of [your] heart will flow rivers of living water" by faith (John 7:38). Where will you share Jesus' *abundant love?* How would the Lord have you take His life-saving message and make a splash with it? Who will be drenched as you do? Imagine those who will be directly affected by the first ring of ripples . . . and the next . . . as they, in turn, have opportunity to share. Soon it has traveled deep and wide in every direction. Pray about your splash and be ready to dive in! Maybe you can

- ♥ listen to someone who needs an advocate—a single mom, a lonely widow, a hurting friend.
- ♥ bring comfort and hope to a hurting family with your meals and your prayers.
- ♥ mentor a young friend, colleague, or neighborhood teen.
- ♥ hold someone accountable who's seeking redirection, assistance, and grace.

♥ step courageously across the room, or across the street, or across town to build a relationship that may open a door to the eventual witness of your faith.

Splash! And what happens from there? Ripple, ripple, ripple. . . . God works powerfully through every action we take, by His grace. Trust that He will carry on your good work through others as the ripples grow outward infinitely.

You are a chosen child of God in Christ, filled to overflowing with God's grace by the Spirit, able to make a splash! Even one drop sends out ripples. Maybe it begins with your impact upon just one other person. Trust that your Savior is able to do far more through you than you can possibly imagine.

JOURNAL

With what will you make a splash? Will it be your kind words, your generous time, your enthusiastic witness? Who has been on your heart? Revisit possibilities shared in this devotion, then journal about the splash and the resulting ripples you'll be able to create as the Lord works through you.

PRAYER

Lord, show me where You would like me to make a splash. Work through me as you work through others, that the ever-expanding ripples may affect the world for Christ . . .

LIMITATIONS

His master said to him, "Well done, good and faithful servant. You have been faithful over a little; I will set you over much. Enter into the joy of your master." Matthew 25:21

I'll never forget my early days as a stay-at-home mom with three little ones underfoot (my twins and my trailer, as I often said). Our days were maxed and messy, and while I loved my vocation, I felt limited in my influence of more people for Jesus and limited in opportunities to serve in our church. I also envied moms whose work took them outside their homes. I lamented all these feelings to my husband, Cory, who validated them and then responded with these unforgettable words: "If our children's souls are the only ones you impact for Christ, and you set your heart to that task, then [like Jesus said], 'Well done, good and faithful servant.' Deb, maybe this is your very purpose!"

Cory borrowed Jesus' words from the parable of the talents. In this parable, the master represents Jesus, and the servants are His followers. The talents represent gifts of great value that Jesus places in His people's care. He teaches us to fully invest in all that God has given us; to faithfully care for the gifts we have received. While Jesus speaks of the *eternal joy* we will have with Him by faith, He also speaks to the blessings we receive in our earthly life as we are faithful with all He entrusts to us for His purposes.

Cory showed me that one of my primary purposes was right in front of my face, but I had missed it while viewing daily life through the lens of limitations. Influencing my children's lives for Christ was paramount to me, just as it was to my fellow working moms who faced unique limitations too. God placed these three gifts of great value in my care. By His grace, I invested in them and trusted that He would do immeasurably more than I could envision for them, and I was humbled to think that He would choose to do His good work through me.

Even when we face limitations, God uses us to reach souls for Christ. God works through our limitations—even despite them. Nothing is wasted in His economy!

How we respond within our limitations—or during a struggle or hardship—speaks loudly to others. Yes, it speaks to our faith, but incomparably more of the grace-filled God we serve!

- Maybe financial limitations mean you can't support an overseas missionary . . . but you can take a bag of groceries to a nearby family in need.

- Maybe your too-full schedule prevents you from volunteering for things you really care about . . . but you can pray for those who do.

- Maybe you can't talk about God at work . . . but you can share His joy through your kind words and actions; you can privately pray for coworkers and be prepared to share Christ when someone asks about the reason for the hope within you (1 Peter 3:15).

You can inspire others right where you are as you live out God's purpose, even (and maybe especially) within your own limitations.

JOURNAL

Write about limitations you have faced within your circumstances. How might God use you, right where you are, to bless others despite your limitations, through them, or because of them? Do you see the many ways He uses you already?

PRAYER

Dear Jesus, thank You for entrusting me with gifts of great value. Lead me to invest in them wisely . . .

PRUNED AND PRODUCING FRUIT

Every branch that does bear fruit He prunes, that it may bear more
fruit. Already you are clean because of the word that I have spoken
to you. Abide in Me, and I in you. As the branch cannot bear fruit
by itself, unless it abides in the vine, neither can you, unless you
abide in Me. I am the vine; you are the branches. Whoever abides
in Me and I in him, he it is that bears much fruit, for apart from Me
you can do nothing. John 15:2–5

As we stared at the ripe berries weighing down the branches, we could
hardly believe it! Weren't these the same overgrown bushes that last
summer had wandered beyond the fence by way of long, skinny shoots? The
bushes had been big then, but had little fruit to show for their size. So, we
trimmed them back last fall. A season later, we were shocked at the bounty.
The more berries we picked, the more we found hiding under the branches.
Our buckets overflowed with the harvest.

The Lord prunes us *out of love*. When we're "trimmed back," it doesn't
always feel like love, especially when it hurts, but because of our daily
struggles with sin, pruning is not only necessary, it also reveals God's overflowing and active love in our lives. We are already cleansed by Christ's forgiveness revealed in His Word (John 15:3). But we are in need of regular
repentance.

Our Father, the gardener (John 15:1), knows exactly when we need to be
cut back because we've been growing in unhealthy directions. Sometimes
we've become stagnant or resistant to healthy growth, so He lops and crops
with precision.

Envision your loving Father, pruning shears in hand, removing
unhealthy branches of envy and impure thoughts; taking away the temp-
tations that lead to idolatry; cutting away weak portions given to jealousy,
anger, and division. (See Galatians 5:19–21.) May we be stripped of every
hindrance for His powerful purpose.

Thanks to the pruning we receive today, we will blossom more bountifully tomorrow and flourish with good fruit in abundance (Galatians 5:22–23), all in the gardener's good time.

Remain in Christ, the true vine. Only as you abide in Jesus will you grow and your life produce the kind of fruit that lasts. Connected to the vine, you are nourished, strengthened, and fruit-*full*, by the Spirit. Not fleeting, worldly, or here today, gone tomorrow, your fruit will feed others, nourish and heal, and assist growth in them too. Your fruit reveals God's active love in you, and He is glorified.

JOURNAL

Describe pruning you have received by God's love and how it helped, even if it was painful at the time. How have you grown as a result, and where do you see blossoms and fruit?

PRAYER

Lord Jesus, You are the vine, and I am merely a branch. Keep me connected to You and produce buckets of fruit in me . . .

HEAD AND HEART

He leads the humble in what is right, and teaches
the humble His way. Psalm 25:9

Well-meaning words stared back at me: "Want to be a better biblical scholar? Study hard. Learn more. Seek answers." This is good advice, if not obvious. Study to learn. Of course. But is it potentially misleading if I believe that growth in my vocations as an author and speaker would come merely with greater intellect and head knowledge?

While it's vital to learn all I can about the Christian faith as I study Bible history, geography, and extrabiblical literature, all the knowledge I acquire intellectually must be peripheral to the centrality of God's Word. Through the *living and active Word of God*, the Holy Spirit speaks, and I am convicted of my sin. I'm also promised forgiveness and new life in my Savior, by God's grace. There in His Word, He teaches me His way (Psalm 25:9), guiding me and causing growth in me, intellectually and spiritually.

In my vocations, may I not forget the primary purpose of all that I do: to glorify God! I pray that my books and my Bible study sessions, combined with His Word, will speak to a person's head and heart. I pray, too, that God, through the Spirit, will strengthen every reader's faith. (Yes, I've prayed for you!) And I pray that He will take my humble offerings and do with them immeasurably more than I can ask for in prayer or imagine in my mind. So, I surrender myself to the Lord daily, trading my attempts to lead by intellect or with cleverly crafted words for His power by the Spirit, so that I may lead others well. May I guide them to growth in Christ, according to the Word.

What's the primary purpose of all that you do, whatever your vocations? As a follower of Jesus, you glorify God too! I'll give those well-meaning words to you:

"Want to be a better _____? Study hard. Learn more. Seek answers." (Again, good advice, if not obvious.) What do you study for your vocations?

Books? People? A craft or skill? Be a lifelong learner; seek answers so you may lead and serve others well in whatever business, ministry, or trade you're led to. Remember, too, that God wants you to study His Word, and not merely for more head knowledge of its richness and promise, but because of the countless ways He will work in you as He speaks to your head and your heart, by every Spirit-inspired word.

Let the Word of Christ dwell in you richly. (Colossians 3:16)

Let it be the central force that shapes, guides, and causes growth in you as it informs every aspect of your life and each vocation. He leads you in what is right and teaches you His ways.

And whatever you do, in word or deed, do everything in the name of the Lord Jesus, giving thanks to God the Father through Him. (Colossians 3:17)

JOURNAL

Write about one or more of your vocations. How can you be a lifelong learner? What does that look like as you seek to serve with your head and your heart and as applied to your study of God's Word?

PRAYER

Lord Jesus, lead me to lifelong learning as I seek to glorify You. Speak to my head and my heart by Your Spirit as I study Your Word . . .

BLESSED → TO BE A BLESSING

You will be enriched in every way to be generous in every way. . . .
For the ministry of this service is not only supplying the needs of
the saints [believers] but is also overflowing in many thanksgiv-
ings to God. 2 Corinthians 9:11–12

Coffee houses today are what soda fountains or corner cafes were to generations past: a popular place to meet for conversation and a treat. Coffee shops are cropping up in bookstores, on college campuses, and in grocery stores. Just the other day, my bank's marquee beckoned, "Come in for our new coffee bar," so I gladly obliged. Coffee shops are opening in churches and thriving across communities. They've become a meeting place for Bible studies, prayer groups, and authentic conversations.

I love my local coffee shops. Would you believe that two are extensions of local churches, ministries to the neighborhoods surrounding them? Each church recognized the needs of the community and God's generous provision of resources, including a unique space for such a gathering place.

Each shop's purpose? To provide a comfortable space for conversation and connection around a cup. God uses these coffee shops for immeasurably more than the founders or baristas could have imagined when they first opened their doors.

They have been blessed → to be a blessing to those they serve—"enriched in every way to be generous in every way." The baristas' warm welcome and generous service fills customers' cups in more ways than one. Friendships grow as acquaintances meet to enjoy camaraderie and coffee. Groups gather for good food, fellowship, and Bible study. Members of the community meet members of the church in casual conversation. Doors are wide open for relationship growth and witness.

In 2 Corinthians 9, Paul commends the Christians in Corinth for their fervor in giving, and he encourages them to continue in their generosity, assuring them of God's *ongoing supply* for all their needs as they continue to pour out for others.

God's grace-filled provision is also true for these coffee shop ministries . . . and for you in your service today. As you give and serve generously, the ministry of your service, like that of the early believers, can create a twofold blessing for those you serve. Through you, God supplies for the needs of His people and He leads them to have hearts overflowing with thanks and praise.

We are blessed ➔ to be a blessing too, and our cups overflow! But instead of sipping from our mugs, what if we poured out abundantly for the benefit of others?

JOURNAL

Name some specific ways you have been blessed. How can your blessings be used to bless others? Brainstorm! Recall past blessings that you've used to bless others.

PRAYER

Lord God, I want to use Your generous provision to bless others in specific ways. Lead the way and I'll follow . . .

PEOPLE-PLEASING

For am I now seeking the approval of man, or of God? Or am I trying to please man? If I were still trying to please man, I would not be a servant of Christ. Galatians 1:10

"No matter what you do, Debbie, not everyone is going to like you." These were wise words from my dad, offered one day when I'd confided through tears how another twelve-year-old had treated me. I didn't know to call it bullying then, but that's what it was. I still need to hear those words today because I still want everyone to like me. People pleasers like me may jump through hoops to prove that we are likable. Maybe you can relate.

Just as I can't make everyone like me no matter what I look like, say, or do, I am faced with another reality: there is just no pleasing people. Period. When I follow a rule just to fit in, I find out the rule has changed. The minute I've switched my wardrobe to follow a fad, styles change and my apparel of choice is so last month. When I adopt the latest technology or download a social media app, I am informed that my device is outdated and the app is passé; I must buy a new device and seek social media connections a different way. I apply current relationship advice, only to learn it's no longer considered relevant. (Maybe my examples are exaggerated, but you get the idea.)

When it comes to pleasing people, I can't win, because the thing that pleases them today may not please them tomorrow. As I am called by God for a purpose, am I called to please others? Or to please God?

More wise words come my way—and yours—from the Lord Himself through the apostle Paul. They concern an incomparably more important issue but can be applied in so many ways. In his letter to the churches in Galatia, Paul scolded the believers; they had fallen for another "gospel," for the rules of men who were distorting the one true Gospel, insisting that Gentile converts to Christianity jump through hoops by being circumcised, just as Jewish converts were. These believers were adding the Law, muddying the purity of the Gospel, and Paul rightly retorted,

> We know that a person is not justified [saved] by works of the law but through faith in Jesus Christ. (Galatians 2:16)

God's eternal purpose is accomplished in Christ (Ephesians 3:11). Covered by His grace, we have His approval! As we consider His purpose for us, we can ask ourselves: Who will God have me meet today? Who will He lead me to call or text regularly? Who is He placing on my heart or in my path so I may listen, lead, and love? He who gives us purpose will be glorified as He uses our humble service, with or without the latest technology, and as we sport fashions that may or may not be *en vogue*. (And, by the way, the best relationship advice is changeless: love them like Jesus does.)

JOURNAL

When have you jumped through a hoop or followed a random rule in an attempt to find favor with others? Choose another question from this devotion to ponder and journal too.

PRAYER

Dear God, please forgive me for trying to please people when I already have Your approval and grace in Christ . . .

FOR WHAT PURPOSE?

I meditate on all that You have done; I ponder the
work of Your hands. Psalm 143:5

Our community just suffered another tragic loss. A teen lost his life in a car accident, and much of the community is mourning. Many are asking why. Understandably so. His family members are followers of Jesus, and they hold on to the certain hope they have in their Savior. Still, the community of believers is asking, "For what purpose did You allow this, Lord?"

Maybe you've asked the same thing. For what purpose . . . ? This painful path of infertility. This senseless act of violence against innocent people. This disaster that left hundreds of families homeless. This heartache that lingers.

When I don't understand how God could allow certain tragedies, struggles, or apparent roadblocks along life's path, I remember that I lack what He does not: perfect vision and a view of the completed scene in the near and distant future. He has foresight and wisdom to know how He will provide during the toughest "for what purpose?" moments . . . and despite them too.

When I am crushed or perplexed, what else can I do? I can remember the Lord's faithfulness in the past. I can "meditate on all that You have done . . . the work of Your hands" (Psalm 143:5). All the while, *He covers me* with His grace and comfort.

God's love for us doesn't lessen or change, even as He has allowed a tough circumstance or season. He doesn't desire any of us to suffer, but we live with the effects of sin in a fallen world. That said, we can be assured that sin doesn't have the final say for all who hope in Him. We can take heart: Jesus has overcome the world (John 16:33). He has rescued you and me for eternity, by God's grace.

For what purpose? He may use our trials to bring us to greater faith as He transforms us through the struggle into the people He is equipping for an opportunity to share His love in Christ.

> We rejoice in our sufferings, knowing that suffering produces endurance, and endurance produces character, and character produces hope, and hope does not put us to shame, because God's love has been poured into our hearts through the Holy Spirit who has been given to us. Romans 5:3–5

We aren't expected to rejoice because of our sufferings, but our Lord is faithful to do immeasurably more than we can comprehend—yes, even in the most difficult times—by the Holy Spirit's power given to us. He will provide us with endurance for the path, despite the roadblocks. He is producing Christlike character in us as a result. And He enables us to hold on to the hope we have in our Savior.

JOURNAL

For what purpose? When might these have been your words? Recall and record the Lord's past faithfulness with specific memories. Personalize this statement: I trust He is faithful to provide me with His grace and comfort as He equips me to _____ with or for someone else in their struggle.

PRAYER

Lord God, sometimes I don't understand for what purpose . . . but I trust Your love and faithfulness . . .

IMMEASURABLY MORE
Peace

YOU GOT THIS!

Do not be anxious about anything, but in everything by prayer and supplication with thanksgiving let your requests be made known to God. And the peace of God, which surpasses all understanding, will guard your hearts and your minds in Christ Jesus. Philippians 4:6–7

A few years ago I was struggling with situational anxiety, hitting roadblocks in ministry, and writer's block in . . . well, writing. *Sigh.* I couldn't shake the anxiety on my own and knew I should lay it in the Lord's hands, but there were days I struggled to do that too. As my children cheered me on and prayed for me, my daughter began texting me: "You got this!" She explained further, "You got this, Mom, but only because God has you in His grip!" She even showered me with thematic gifts to serve as constant reminders! My boys caught on and joined her. Even now, when I ask for personal prayer, especially as it involves anxiety over an issue, a struggle, or a roadblock, they respond with our own prayer-peace code: "You got this, Mom!"

In my ongoing battle with anxiety, I remember this: *The God of peace is with me always.* I pray that my eyes may be open to recognize His presence right in the middle of whatever anxious circumstance I'm living in. His timely provision; His creative, restorative power; His sunrise, seen with new appreciation; His answer of peace when I've cried to Him in confusion; and His promise to work all things together for good (see Romans 8:28). So I pray as Philippians 4:6 directs, "with thanksgiving"—with a heart full of thanks to God for taking care of my anxiety and me, even when I don't know how He will answer.

As my daughter said, God has me in His grip. It's true! He has you there too.

[Cast] all your anxieties on Him, because He cares for you. (1 Peter 5:7)

As we take every anxious thought to God—from the smallest to the greatest care—we can trust Him to trade it for His peace. He guards our hearts and our minds in our Savior, Jesus, providing immeasurably more peace than we can ask for or imagine.

Hearts and minds that are guarded by the peace of God may be fixed on whatever is worthy of praise, as we fix our thoughts on these things—on anything and everything that is true, honorable, just, pure, lovely, and more (Philippians 4:8). And that's not all! By God's grace, we can live out what we're learning, putting every "whatever" into practice (v. 9)! This, too, is God's work, as He does immeasurably more, in answer to our anxious cries.

JOURNAL

"You got this" might sound silly, but thanks to my kids, it's really a prayer-peace code, reminding me to take my anxious thoughts to the One who can trade them for His peace (and more)! Write about or create a word picture that leads you to prayer when you're feeling anxious. Share it with loved ones who can use the code with you when you need the same reminder.

PRAYER

Dear God, thank You for guarding my heart and my mind with Your peace. Lead me to take everything to you in prayer . . .

HE KEEPS COUNT

You have kept count of my tossings; put my tears in Your bottle. Are they not in Your book? Psalm 56:8

I tossed and turned last night. My mind played yesterday's car accident on repeat. If only I had turned the wheel differently, I could have regained control. If only I hadn't panicked at the sight of oncoming traffic, my car's front end might not have made contact with the tree. I wasn't injured and the car will be repaired. As accidents go, this one was minor. So why wasn't I able to rest? Why did the tears flow so freely? Our friend was in a car accident the day before, sustaining a concussion and receiving staples to his head. His accident was far worse, and the guilt I felt over my own was coupled with thoughts like "Why are you so upset? Next to others, your problems are nothing." Wait. Was that true?

Your problems matter to God because *you are precious to Him*. And maybe your problem is vastly different, bigger, or smaller than mine. Comparison isn't healthy and doesn't help. The truth is, when pain penetrates your heart, the Lord hurts for you and with you. Be honest in your cries when you don't understand His timing or His plan or something He has allowed to happen. Even if your answer doesn't arrive when or how you expect it, you can trust that He is working. He is your strength when you are weak and weepy. He is your help in every trial and trouble (Psalm 46:1). He will answer according to His perfect will and give you His peace.

Pray the psalmist's words in Psalm 56:8 (above). After all, the Lord keeps count of your tossings too. Those restless nights when you toss and turn? He watches over you (Psalm 121:3–4)! He understands the ache in your heart. He walks with you through the pain you've sustained. And He knows every tear you've cried.

The eyes of the LORD are toward the righteous and His ears toward their cry.... When the righteous cry for help, the LORD hears and delivers them out of all their troubles. Psalm 34:15, 17

We can trust the Lord to use our troubles for good. While we don't have to slap on a smiley face and fake how we feel when we're struggling, we can admit that our growth is often most evident in times of trouble. And even if our problems persist, we can cling to the faith we profess: Jesus is our Savior. He keeps count of our tears, but not our sins. He took those with Him to the cross and forgave us for every one of them.

By God's grace through faith, you and I possess the resurrection power of Jesus (Ephesians 1:19–20), which enables us to face heartache head-on and pain with perseverance. By faith, we also possess His peace, the peace that surpasses our own understanding or lack thereof.

We are not alone, and I believe we are richer for having faced difficult circumstances. We cling to God's words such as these:

Count it all joy, my brothers, when you meet trials of various kinds, for you know that the testing of your faith produces steadfastness. And let steadfastness have its full effect, that you may be perfect and complete, lacking in nothing. (James 1:2–4)

JOURNAL

Share your problems with the One who keeps count of your tossings and tears. When have you witnessed your growth or others' in a troubled time?

PRAYER

Lord God, You have kept count of my tossings; You've put my tears in Your bottle. I thank and praise You for Your care . . .

A LITTLE PEACE AND QUIET

Since we have been justified by faith, we have peace with God through
our Lord Jesus Christ. Romans 5:1

Is it too much to ask for a little peace and quiet?! (It's okay to admit
you've said this . . . or at least thought it!) Perhaps peace eludes you as
you attempt to juggle your work schedule, children, and chores! Maybe
moments of quiet are out of your grasp as you stare at a full calendar, field
chaotic demands at work and home, or mediate between squabbling siblings. So, you'd just like a minute of peace and quiet. Or, you think that
peace is elusive for reasons beyond your grasp: cultural unrest, social division, and violence across the country and around the world.

Because of sin, this world does not and cannot know true peace or quiet.

So, God sent a Savior into this sin-ridden world. The prophet Isaiah
foretold that a child would be born to us, that He would be called
"Wonderful Counselor, Mighty God, Everlasting Father, Prince of Peace"
(Isaiah 9:6). That child, God's own Son, would deliver true and lasting peace
to the world.

Isaiah prophesied that the Messiah would restore Israel. This long-
awaited deliverer would bring peace and supply all their needs. This and
every prophecy were perfectly fulfilled in Christ, who came, but not as the
people envisioned. He arrived, not as a warrior king like His ancestor David,
but as a lowly infant, our Suffering Servant, the Prince of Peace whose sinless life and sacrificial death provided perfect peace for you and me. Isaiah
foretold:

He was pierced for our transgressions; He was crushed for our iniquities; upon Him was the chastisement that brought us peace, and with
His wounds we are healed. (Isaiah 53:5)

You receive true peace with God through faith in Christ. He extends His
peace to you, even into your work-a-day world where you may fail to feel an

ounce of peace. Despite your days, remember that *in Jesus, you have true peace that is incomparably greater than anything the world offers*:

> Peace I leave with you; My peace I give to you. Not as the world gives do I give to you. (John 14:27)

When peace and quiet elude you, remember His peace that is yours by the Spirit (Galatians 5:22), His righteousness that is yours by faith. Isaiah 32 speaks of both, concerning the Spirit being poured upon us (v. 15).

> And the effect of righteousness will be peace, and the result of righteousness, quietness and trust forever. My people will abide in a peaceful habitation, in secure dwellings, and in quiet resting places. (Isaiah 32:17–18)

One day, when Christ returns, we will know perfect peace and quiet, and it will be indescribably better than all we could ask for or imagine.

JOURNAL

For what reasons do you seek a little peace and quiet? In what ways does peace appear elusive to you? Read John 14:27 again, and describe Jesus' peace in your own words.

PRAYER

Jesus, Your peace is like no other. Thank You for the perfect peace and quiet that will one day be mine, in eternity with You . . .

FOOTHOLDS

The LORD will be your confidence and will keep your foot from being caught. Proverbs 3:26

A foothold is a good thing if you're climbing. Finding a foothold is essential for security, so you can take the next step, confident you won't slip. But let's turn this word around and apply it the way we often hear it, as in, when something "has a foothold" on us. Like fear.

How does fear attempt to have a foothold on you? What may cause you to be gripped with fear? Maybe you're facing a loved one's medical diagnosis or you're embarking on a new career. You stare into new surroundings or you're not sure how you'll make ends meet. You fear a friend's response if you dare to share your faith. You fear the future every time you turn on the TV.

The Lord speaks frequently to fear across Scripture because He knows our battles and He provides for our needs. Jesus Himself says repeatedly, "Do not be afraid." He says it not to chastise the people He encounters, but to calm and comfort them, to reassure His beloved that even before they speak, He knows when they are afraid.

Perfect love drives out fear (1 John 4:18). Christ was driven by His perfect love for us when He courageously climbed Calvary's hill and faced the cross in our place. There, *He conquered every sin* that had its foothold on us. Removing fear's grip, He makes our steps secure (Psalm 40:2).

He knows every fearful thought just as He knows our needs. Jesus' love casts out our fear—removes its foothold—and replaces it with His peace. We have His Word on it.

- We fear death, but Jesus says, "I am the resurrection and the life. Whoever believes in Me, though he die, yet shall he live, and everyone who lives and believes in Me shall never die" (John 11:25–26).

- We fear being alone and Jesus says, "I am with you always, to the end of the age" (Matthew 28:20).

- When we're afraid of what our enemies will do to us, we can say with the psalmist, "In God I trust; I shall not be afraid. What can man do to me?" (Psalm 56:11).

- And when we fear that we are not loved, we read these words, "See what kind of love the Father has given to us, that we should be called children of God; and so we are" (1 John 3:1).

God speaks to every kind of fear with reassurance for us. After all, God has His grip upon us, and no other foothold can compare with His might!

Fear not, for I am with you; be not dismayed, for I am your God; I will strengthen you, I will help you, I will uphold you with My righteous right hand. (Isaiah 41:10)

JOURNAL

What fears attempt to have a foothold on you? Share here. Write out a verse from this devotion (or elsewhere) that gives you a good word of peace concerning these fears.

PRAYER

Lord, You are mightier than my fears. Strengthen me, help me, and uphold me with Your righteous right hand . . .

CRY OUT TO GOD

How long, O Lord? Will You forget me forever? How long will You hide Your face from me? How long must I take counsel in my soul and have sorrow in my heart all the day? . . . But I have trusted in Your steadfast love; my heart shall rejoice in Your salvation. I will sing to the Lord, because He has dealt bountifully with me. Psalm 13:1–2, 5–6

What's causing you stress or stealing your peace? Maybe you've been anxious about something for a long time, and you're weary of bringing it to the Lord in prayer. Maybe it feels like He has forgotten you or your pleas for help. What if someone has hurt you or something has threatened your hope? Maybe you cannot see how God could use a situation—or you—for good. Whenever your thoughts or circumstances threaten to steal your peace, cry out to the Lord.

Several years ago, my husband guided me to King David's song of lament in Psalm 13 for comfort in such times. Since then, I've guided several stressed and worried women to these words. The Lord God knows your thoughts and your circumstances already. Tell Him all that troubles you. Give it to Him straight, even if your feelings would have you frustrated, wondering where God is or if He has heard you. Yes, even when your feelings don't line up with the absolute truth of God's Word, you can confide in Him, complain to Him, and confess these feelings as you cry out. Like David, you can come to God's throne of grace with confidence, admitting your anger, your uncertainty, and all that's stressing you today! *Trust His mercy* for you in Christ. Know that He holds the answers, the future, and you.

Let us then with confidence draw near to the throne of grace,
that we may receive mercy and find grace to help in time of
need. (Hebrews 4:16)

David's God-given trust enabled him to courageously cry out first. That same trust led his heart to rejoice and his mouth to sing praise. He praised God for what he knew to be true:

- God's steadfast love
- God's salvation
- God's bountiful provision

Follow your cries with praise, speaking God's truth right back to Him. Praise Him for His love, and rejoice in His salvation that's yours by faith in Christ. Recall specific ways He has dealt bountifully with you, providing hope and help, according to your needs.

Trust God to trade your burdens for His peace. He has not forgotten you. He can do what you cannot, so trust Him to do immeasurably more as He works through your situation—and through you—for good and His glory. Rest, reassured of God's promises and His bountiful provision of peace.

JOURNAL

What's the source of your anxiety, stress, or weariness? Use David's heart cries in Psalm 13 as a guide to share your heart with the Lord. Write about God's past provision. What has He done for you, by His might, that you could not have done alone?

PRAYER

O Lord, I have trusted in Your steadfast love; my heart rejoices in Your salvation. I will sing to You because You have dealt bountifully with me . . .

WHICH WAY?

Jesus said . . . , "I am the way, and the truth, and the life. No one comes to the Father except through Me." John 14:6

Should I choose A or B? Lord, please show me!

I'm often looking for clear direction. I'm sure you are too. I waver between options, wondering why the Lord doesn't skywrite an obvious answer to me! (Sometimes He does provide the clear guidance that I'm watching for, but other times I'm left wondering.) I let indecision become a burden, a cause of anxious thoughts, a thief of my peace. When I don't recognize or receive an obvious answer to the direction I seek, I start to panic: *What if I choose poorly? How will I know I'm following God's lead and not just forcing a trail I've determined to follow?* Yikes!

Praise God for the counsel He provides in His Word and via godly mentors. When both (or all) options point in a positive direction and when no option raises red flags (warnings that it could lead me away from God's truth), I can trust that I have His blessing and His guiding hand every step of the way. If I should stumble off the path and down a dangerous trail, He doesn't leave me to fend for myself. By His grace, He guides me back.

Wherever I go, *His hand holds mine*. In fact, there is nowhere you or I can go apart from His presence. King David said that even if he should settle in the farthest part of the sea,

> Even there Your hand shall lead me, and Your right hand shall hold me. (Psalm 139:10)

Can I trust that God will use my prayerful, careful decision for the work He already has in mind? Do I believe He will work through me to do immeasurably more than all that I ask or imagine? Yes and yes!

I want to receive the counsel of the Lord as Isaiah instructs: "And your ears shall hear a word behind you, saying, 'This is the way, walk in it,' when you turn to the right or when you turn to the left" (Isaiah 30:21). While I wish that He would whisper in my ear, "Go right!" "Turn left!" maybe the plan He has for me allows for either turn.

One thing is even clearer than skywriting: He has provided the way in Jesus (John 14:6). So, I pray with every decision that the direction I take will please God, point others to Christ, and give Him glory.

JOURNAL

What fork in the road have you come to where you've wondered, "Which way?" What was the outcome? Using guidance from this devotion, write about a decision you may be facing today.

PRAYER

Dear Jesus, You are the way! Lead me to decisions that please You and point others to You too . . .

OUT OF CONTROL

For My thoughts are not your thoughts, neither are your ways My ways, declares the Lord. For as the heavens are higher than the earth, so are My ways higher than your ways and My thoughts than your thoughts. Isaiah 55:8–9

"Surely," I say to myself, "peace will come when I get over this hurdle . . . or check that task off the list . . . or seize control of the things that attempt to control me . . . or . . ." I lose peace (and sleep) over my schedule, responsibilities, writing tasks, and more. Even as I attempt to grasp peace by gaining control over all parts of these matters, I do so in vain. True peace cannot be found in this kind of control, and lasting peace is not mine when I've leapt a hurdle without falling on my face. (Inevitably, there's another hurdle ahead. *Sigh*.) And that daunting task on my to-do list that I successfully checked? It will be replaced by five more anyway.

Only as God reminds me again in His Word that He has control over all things do I remember that true inner peace is already mine by faith in Christ. So-called peace would continually elude me, even if I maintained my meager attempts at achieving it. So, I lay my will and my ways before the Lord. His thoughts and *His ways outshine mine* every day of the week, and I trust that my time (including my schedule) is in His hands (Psalm 31:15). Even when I don't think I can write another word or complete another task, I trust that He is able to do immeasurably more . . . according to His power at work in me, for someone else's good and for His glory. I want to make the best use of every responsibility, each task, and the time I am given, but I trust the Lord to establish my steps.

The heart of man plans his way, but the Lord establishes his steps. (Proverbs 16:9)

By the Lord's power, along with His prevalent peace, you and I take each step in faith. We may be out of control, but He never is. And the peace of God is peace with God: reconciliation through Jesus.

For in Him all the fullness of God was pleased to dwell, and through Him to reconcile to Himself all things, whether on earth or in heaven, making peace by the blood of His cross. (Colossians 1:19–20)

True peace is ours in the One who truly has control.

And God be praised, for even as I lose sleep over my writing, even as I toss and turn with worry, I receive a good Word of peace from the Lord, and good words from someone who told me, "Don't stop writing. God is using your work." While we often don't see where He is working, sometimes He shows us a glimpse. To God be the glory!

JOURNAL

Compare and contrast peace that the world offers with God's promise of peace in Christ. Share an example of a good word you have received from someone just when you needed it.

PRAYER

Lord God, forgive me for attempting to take control. Establish my steps for others' good and for Your glory . . .

BROKEN DREAMS

The LORD is near to the brokenhearted and saves the
crushed in spirit. Psalm 34:18

"Life wasn't supposed to turn out this way."

"This isn't where I saw myself."

"My dream was shattered . . ."

In the face of frustration, collapsing plans, disappointment, or broken
dreams, we've said similar things, haven't we? While we stare at something
torn to pieces, God looks with compassion upon us and our broken bits. He
"is near to the brokenhearted and saves the crushed in spirit." He picks up
the scraps of what remains—every single shard—and He repurposes them,
creating something new. He does that with us too.

He heals the brokenhearted and binds up their wounds. (Psalm 147:3)

Even greater, He heals our brokenness in Christ.

But He was pierced for our transgressions; He was crushed for our iniquities; upon Him was the chastisement that brought us peace, and with
His wounds we are healed. (Isaiah 53:5)

Because something in life didn't turn out the way we had hoped, do we
start to assume that God will not or cannot use us in today's context? Of
course not. Does He hear our woes and receive us with compassion? Every
moment of every day. Sometimes, we put God in a proverbial box, lim-
iting the ways we believe He may choose to work or placing limits upon the
scope of that work.

The Lord's plan and knowledge of the completed picture of that plan far
supersede ours because we only see the messy middle. The apostle Paul's
imagery in 1 Corinthians 13:12 speaks to this: "For now we see in a mirror
dimly, but then face to face. Now I know in part; then I shall know fully,

even as I have been fully known." Even now, Jesus sees and knows us fully. When He returns, we will see Him face to face and understand fully too. But for now, we only know in part. We see dimly at best. And sometimes the image is skewed or at least limited.

Maybe a plan that was important to you fell through, but that doesn't mean God's purpose is thwarted. His purpose will stand (Proverbs 19:21). Pray that your pain or disappointment draws you into deeper fellowship with Him and with someone who could use your understanding and compassion. Maybe they stare at similar shattered dreams, frustrating setbacks, or letdowns. How can you bear their burden (Galatians 6:2) and reassure them of Christ's peace?

Broken dreams do not have to prevent us from dreaming. Because God continues His good work in us, He is still able to do immeasurably more than we could imagine in our wildest dreams! Where we see brokenness, God is working out healing and peace. *We have His promise* that as we cast our life's burdens on Him, He will sustain us (Psalm 55:22). The life God has for you in Christ—now and for eternity—is greater than your greatest disappointment or shattered dream. In the place of your broken dreams, He provides peace.

JOURNAL

If you are faced with a broken dream, how could the fulfilled prophecy of Isaiah 53:5 give you peace? How may God repurpose a shattered dream to create something new?

PRAYER

Lord Jesus, by Your wounds, I am healed. Draw me closer to You and give me Your peace . . .

PERFECT PEACE

You keep him in perfect peace whose mind is stayed on You,
because he trusts in You. Isaiah 26:3

I'm seeking peace today. Let me count the ways . . .

I'm sure I'll find serenity as I scroll through social media or go shopping. I'll pamper myself with a pedicure. Even better, I'll calm myself with a cup of cocoa or a hot latte. Perfect! (Mmm . . . the aroma and ambiance awaiting me at my favorite coffee shop are certain to provide peace.)

I confess, these are my favorite go-to pleasures, my means of escape when my mind is on overload and anxious thoughts threaten. I'm craving peace and I run after it, hoping I'll catch a little peace of mind, serenity, or release.

While most of my go-to attempts aren't inherently poor choices, they provide a false sense of peace, a fleeting release. They offer less than what my heart and mind truly crave. The peace you and I need is the perfect peace we receive by the Holy Spirit (Galatians 5:22) that surpasses our limited level of human understanding. It's deeper than intellect or surface-level recognition, and it's incomparably better than some fleeting, feel-good pleasure found in a cup or a screen. God guards us—heart and mind—with *His perfect peace* (Philippians 4:7).

When Jesus gathered His disciples in the Upper Room just before His arrest, He spoke to the anxious thoughts that threatened them already and to their fears that would only escalate in following days. Preparing them for His arrest and death, and pointing them to His resurrection and ascension into heaven, He consoled them. He does the same for us today:

Peace I leave with you; My peace I give to you. Not as the world gives do I give to you. Let not your hearts be troubled, neither let them be afraid. (John 14:27)

When Jesus spoke in this verse of the peace the world gives, He didn't mean what planet earth provides or all that dwells within it, though every part of creation is a good gift from God. By *world*, He meant the external and fleeting things—the trinkets, trappings, and treasures—of this world. None of these can provide the peace we seek either.

Do not lay up for yourselves treasures on earth, where moth and rust destroy and where thieves break in and steal, but lay up for yourselves treasures in heaven, where neither moth nor rust destroys and where thieves do not break in and steal. For where your treasure is, there your heart will be also. (Matthew 6:19–21)

What will we treasure? Where will our hearts and minds find focus? In the fleeting, earthly things, or in the eternal treasures promised by God in Christ? May He keep us in perfect peace as our minds stay on our Savior, as we trust in Him.

JOURNAL

What worldly pleasures or means of escape have you employed in an attempt to find true or lasting peace? What makes God's peace perfect?

PRAYER

Dear God, please keep constant guard over my heart and my mind in Christ Jesus. Lead me to focus on Your eternal treasures . . .

IN DARKNESS AND DIFFICULTY

So Peter got out of the boat and walked on the water and came to
Jesus. But when he saw the wind, he was afraid, and beginning to
sink he cried out, "Lord, save me." Jesus immediately reached out
His hand and took hold of him, saying to him, "O you of little faith,
why did you doubt?" And when they got into the boat, the wind
ceased. And those in the boat worshiped Him, saying, "Truly You are
the Son of God." Matthew 14:29–33

More than five thousand people headed for home with satisfied stomachs, thanks to a miraculous meal that followed Jesus' teaching and healing. At dusk on that day, Jesus instructed His disciples to go ahead of Him by boat onto the Sea of Galilee while He withdrew alone to pray. Later in the evening, winds rose, a storm raged, and waves beat against the boat. The disciples faced darkness and difficulty throughout the night.

In the wee hours of the next morning, before dawn, Jesus appeared to them, walking toward His disciples on the water. They cried out in fear, certain they were seeing a ghost. Then Jesus spoke: "It is I. Do not be afraid." Peter was so relieved that it was Jesus that he left the relative safety of the boat to join Him on the roiling water. For a short time, Peter accomplished the impossible; by Jesus' power he walked on water too. Then he remembered the storm. Peter panicked and cried out to Jesus, who reached for His frightened follower and brought him into the boat. And the storm stopped.

We face dark times and difficult nights . . . and days. Jesus speaks into the darkness and difficulties of life, and He not only speaks, He acts. For so many reasons, we cry out in fear, and *Jesus meets us there*. He speaks into our lives: "Do not be afraid. It is I." "I am the way, and the truth, and the life" (John 14:6). "I am the resurrection and the life" (John 11:25). He comes to us, walks with us, even accomplishes the impossible through us! He forgives us for our faltering faith, reaches out His hand, and takes hold of us, again and again.

When dark times and difficult storms swirl around and within us, we cry out, "Lord, save us!" And already, He is there. He pulls us up and draws us to Himself. He who *is* our peace provides peace by His presence amid every circumstance.

Reach for me, Jesus. Hold me. Be my peace.

JOURNAL

Read Matthew 14:22–33 for the full story on the stormy Sea of Galilee, and envision the disciples' dark and difficult time. How can you apply Jesus' words and actions to your darkness and difficulty?

PRAYER

Lord, save me! Reach for me, Jesus. Hold me. Be my peace . . .

IMMEASURABLY MORE
Joy

RECEIVING JESUS JOYFULLY

[Zacchaeus] was a chief tax collector and was rich. And he was seeking to see who Jesus was, but on account of the crowd he could not, because he was small in stature. So he ran on ahead and climbed up into a sycamore tree to see Him, for He was about to pass that way. Luke 19:2–4

I'm so glad Zacchaeus climbed a sycamore tree. This wee little man (Are you singing yet?) longed to see who Jesus was. He had heard about Jesus.

Zacchaeus was known by his peers as a cheating tax collector, employed by Rome. He may have taken a risk showing up that day. Maybe he climbed the tree for a reason other than to gain a better view than his small stature would allow—the Bible doesn't tell us—but maybe that tree offered a little safety from the crowd because he knew he wasn't welcome. He hoped only to get a glimpse of Jesus, but Jesus came his way that day to give Zacchaeus immeasurably more. Jesus saw him. More than merely spotting a man hidden in a tree, Jesus truly *saw* Zacchaeus. He knew who Zacchaeus was, called him by name, and called him down from that sycamore tree. Then He invited Himself into Zacchaeus's home and life.

Jesus . . . looked up and said to him, "Zacchaeus, hurry and come down, for I must stay at your house today." So he hurried and came down and received [Jesus] joyfully. (Luke 19:5–6)

Jesus knew Zacchaeus's sin; He also knew his heart. And that day, He gave a sinful man forgiveness and a fresh start. With joy, Zacchaeus received Jesus, hurrying to be there!

While we don't deserve Jesus' attention in our direction either, we also receive immeasurably more! He comes to us and truly knows us . . . our sins and our repentant hearts. *Our Savior sought and saved us* when we were lost; He called us by name in our Baptism, forgave us, and formed a relationship with us. (And yes, He's in our homes with us every day!) May we continually respond as Zacchaeus did that day, receiving Jesus joyfully too.

We see evidence of Jesus' work in this tax collector's heart; he offered to give half of all he owned to the poor and to restore fourfold to all whom he had cheated. And Jesus said to him, "Today salvation has come to this house. . . . For the Son of Man came to seek and to save the lost" (Luke 19:9–10).

As Jesus daily works in my heart, may I continually be changed by His grace, so that with boundless joy, I seek to set right where I have wronged others and give where I have formerly taken. I pray that He may do immeasurably more . . . according to His power at work in me. To God be the glory!

JOURNAL

Read the full story of Jesus and Zacchaeus in Luke 19:1–10 from the perspective of the crowd or Zacchaeus or Jesus. Write what stands out to you. How do you receive Jesus joyfully?

PRAYER

Lord Jesus, thank You for seeking and saving me. May I rejoice in You every day . . .

EVERY MOMENT MATTERS

*When anxiety was great within me, Your consolation
brought me joy. Psalm 94:19, NIV*

I fretted that I wasn't doing enough to lead my growing children in our family's walk with Jesus. Devotion time went by the wayside more often than not. What we established while they were young became increasingly difficult to continue with consistency when commitments increased with each season. I guilted myself, knowing those were just excuses. More to the point: our efforts were weak, and we often missed the mark to keep the attention of our adolescent children. But God knew our anxious hearts and forgave us for our shortcomings, as He heard our ongoing prayers. He consoled us and provided answers in many and unexpected ways. He was working in our kids: They posed faith-based questions from the passenger seats during long drives. They took an interest in Christian music and examined the messages within the lyrics. They were blessed with the influence of other godly adults and families around them. We learned that every moment mattered, not just the ones we had expected to make a difference. Joy was evident in our home and in our growing children.

Instead of berating our waning efforts toward our once-cherished family devotion time, my husband and I found joy in the evidence of our children's growing faith: their intriguing commentaries following a Sunday sermon, their insightful questions regarding a peer's comment or choice. God was moving in and through them via unexpected and various means. We were humbled and overjoyed at His continual work that far surpassed our efforts.

Perhaps you're raising children right now, praying similarly, but anxiously awaiting answers. Or maybe you're not a parent, but you want to influence a loved one's faith walk, and you believe your efforts have fallen short. You've wondered how or when you will recognize growth. *Trust God.* He knows the anxiety within you; His consolation will bring you joy. He will provide answers, often in unexpected ways. So pray to the One who knows what is best, gives generously, and does immeasurably more than we can ask through our humble prayers as He works in and through them for others' good and for His glory.

> We have not ceased to pray for you, asking that you may be filled with the knowledge of His will in all spiritual wisdom and understanding, so as to walk in a manner worthy of the Lord, fully pleasing to Him: bearing fruit in every good work and increasing in the knowledge of God; being strengthened with all power, according to His glorious might, for all endurance and patience with joy; giving thanks to the Father. . . . He has . . . transferred us to the kingdom of His beloved Son, in whom we have redemption, the forgiveness of sins. (Colossians 1:9–14)

May God grant that we are family members and friends who abide with Jesus.

May we grow in His Word, where He prepares us for every unexpected conversation and every teachable moment . . . because every moment matters (including but not limited to family devotion time). Through it, He does immeasurably more.

JOURNAL

Concerning a friend or family member's faith, how have you fretted? Are you anxiously awaiting answers? When have you also been overjoyed at evidence of God's work?

PRAYER

Dear Lord God, I trust Your continued work in my loved ones and in me. Thank You for using every moment for Your good . . .

JOY IN CHAINS

We rejoice in our sufferings, knowing that suffering produces endurance, and endurance produces character, and character produces hope, and hope does not put us to shame, because God's love has been poured into our hearts through the Holy Spirit who has been given to us. Romans 5:3–5

Feet fastened in stocks, Paul and Silas sat on the cold prison floor of Philippi, surrounded by criminals facing a similar fate. But these missionaries had been wrongly arrested following false accusations as they proclaimed the Gospel in this city. They'd endured beatings, and were thrown into prison to suffer further. In that dark cell, however, a sweet sound arose. Paul and Silas prayed and sang songs of praise to the Lord, whose message they proclaimed (Acts 16:25). Their *joy in Christ* spilled out of them and onto everyone within earshot, and God would soon do immeasurably more through their humble praises than they could have expected, as the Spirit sang through them. Suddenly there was a great earthquake, so that the foundations of the prison were shaken. And immediately all the doors were opened, and everyone's bonds were unfastened (Acts 16:26).

Following the earthquake, every prisoner remained, though their bonds had been broken. Paul called out to the jailer and saved him from taking his own life.

God's love working through them, Paul and Silas gained the jailer and his entire family for Christ. They baptized and spoke the Word of the Lord to the entire household, and the jailer responded in joy by the Spirit's power! He rejoiced along with his entire household that he had believed in God (Acts 16:34).

Ten years later, Paul was chained again, this time in Rome. Writing to the church in Philippi, he was quick to tell the Philippian believers that God was using his circumstances for good.

I want you to know, brothers, that what has happened to me has really served to advance the gospel. (Philippians 1:12)

God would do immeasurably more through Paul's sufferings than even Paul could see (and his eyes were wide with hope). Paul's imprisonment emboldened fellow Christians to speak the Word fearlessly, and Paul's joy in Jesus extended exponentially: throughout Rome (vv. 13–14), to the first readers in Philippi, and to countless people through the centuries, including you and me. We can proclaim as Paul, "Christ is proclaimed, and in that I rejoice!" (v. 18). Paul could rejoice even in persecution; God chose to use him to witness for Christ.

Although we may never know chains, you and I face sufferings too. We may wonder how we can possibly rejoice amid certain circumstances. We may not have the opportunity to see firsthand, as Paul did, some of the ways God will use our trial, suffering, or struggle. Then again, maybe we will. Regardless, we hold on to His promise, confident that He is at work. We can rejoice, trusting that He will produce endurance → character → and hope in us. Confident in the hope that is Christ, we can boldly ask Him to do more than we can imagine, "through the Holy Spirit who has been given to us," to praise God and proclaim His name.

JOURNAL

Imagine Paul's overwhelming joy as he saw God use circumstances for good, to bring even the unlikely to faith. In what circumstance has this devotion found you today? Imagine—if you can't yet see—how God will use a past or current situation for good. Write your imaginings.

PRAYER

Dear God, enable me to hold on to Your promises and rejoice, even in suffering, because You are faithful . . .

SURPRISED BY JOY

Be glad in the Lord, and rejoice, O righteous, and shout for joy, all
you upright in heart! Psalm 32:11

While vacationing on Hawaii's Big Island, my family scheduled a snorkeling adventure. Secretly afraid to go, I put on a brave face and set out
with everyone via two-person kayaks. All the way to our coral reef destination, I worried. I offered up silent prayers as we paddled amid the rough
waves. Upon our arrival, I told myself I would just watch from the kayak
while my husband and children snorkeled. Cory successfully exited the
floating vessel, but when he attempted to come aboard again, we tipped to
the side and—surprise!—suddenly I was in the water. On our next attempt,
the kayak flipped over entirely and bonked my head. Wet and frazzled
(but not concussed), I decided, "Why not try snorkeling? I've been through
worse already."

I. Loved. It. Directly beneath me lay a remarkable expanse of coral reef
decorated with schools of brilliant blue and yellow fish. The wonder in this
glimpse of God's oceanic creation gripped me. I had almost missed it.

When are you secretly (or not-so-secretly) afraid to try something new?
To take a calculated risk?

Pray. Ask God to give you more than a brave face; allow His power to
work in and through you, even when your waves are rough, and just keep
paddling. And praying. You can expect Him to do immeasurably more than
you ask or think.

May we not merely watch as others bask in the joy of God's creation,
provision, and beauty—let's jump in and join them! (His joy is yours in Jesus,
whether you exit the boat or not. So, rejoice!) Even the roaring sea proclaims the joy of the Lord, by His handiwork in all that fills it!

Let the heavens be glad, and let the earth rejoice; let the sea roar, and
all that fills it. (Psalm 96:11)

But how often does God allow a tip, a flip, even a knock upside the head so we won't miss the joy, the wonder, the spectacular view, or breathtaking moment He reveals right in front of (or beneath) us? All so we may glorify Him and tell of His wonders!

Where may God surprise you with joy? Sometimes He allows you to be tipped over, upset, even bonked on the head to reveal His *more* for you. May we rejoice in the Lord—even shout for joy—in every surprise, in every test, and in every trial (James 1:2) because He has made us righteous in Christ and He is growing our faith. He forgives our worries, fears, and failures to trust. Even when our proverbial boats tip or flip, we remain "upright in heart," by His grace.

JOURNAL

Write about a time you have been secretly (or not-so-secretly) afraid to try something new or take a calculated risk. Ponder where God may surprise you with joy next.

PRAYER

Lord God, when I'm afraid, fill me with Your courage and power. Sometimes Your joy takes me by surprise, but it's always mine in Christ . . .

DELIGHT!

*This is the day that the LORD has made; let us rejoice
and be glad in it. Psalm 118:24*

My dad tells the story of three-year-old Debbie on one particular day. I was humming a happy tune while making pie-pies (mud pies) in my outdoor play kitchen, complete with an old oven. He walked up just as I was peeking into the oven and overheard my squeal of delight, "They're just about done!" My dad witnessed his little girl making "pies" like her mom and squealing with unrestrained joy! Do I delight so readily today? What if today looks like all mud and no pie?

Now that you and I are all grown up, our days are filled with responsibilities and cares that may crowd out any opportunity to play pretend, let alone squeal with delight. We live out days that are heavy or ho-hum at least. *Sigh.* I think we could use a shot in the arm right about now. Ready?

Today is yet another day the Lord has made.

What can we do? "Rejoice and be glad in it." Rejoice that salvation in Christ is ours. Be glad for another day to share it!

Maybe I only want to rejoice despite the day or after it is over. Nevertheless, I'm called to *be glad and rejoice in it*; this day that God has made is ultimately good because God is good. All the time. Every. Day. Therefore, I rejoice, whatever the day holds. God did exceedingly more in Paul's prison days, David's hiding days, and Moses' staff-bearing days than all they could have asked or imagined. God was working right in the midst of their difficult days, and He is doing the same for you and me.

Joy is ours every day. Unlike happiness, joy is not contingent upon our circumstances, and we don't have to manufacture it. Joy is ours in Christ, a fruit that flows out of faith.

The fruit of the Spirit is love, joy, peace . . . (Galatians 5:22)

Chosen by Christ and by the work of the Holy Spirit, we possess joy, whether we notice it on a given day or not. What could we do daily with the joy we are given? Will we allow it to overflow for the world to see? How can we bear and share this fruit of the Spirit?

Watch for reasons to delight, right in the middle of life: Take time to smell the proverbial roses (or the real ones). Don't wait for the weekend to make a favorite meal, and savor each flavor . . . or make a pie, like my mom does! Expect to see a few smiles in return when you offer one freely. A twinkle in your eyes can bring joy to someone's heart:

The light of the eyes rejoices the heart. (Proverbs 15:30)

Look expectantly for opportunities to impact your world for Christ, one heart at a time. Delight in God's Word today, knowing that He speaks to you. Then trust Him to do immeasurably more, by Jesus' joy in you!

JOURNAL

In what ways do you (or could you) delight daily? Ponder ways you can let Jesus' joy overflow onto someone in a tangible way.

PRAYER

Lord God, this is another day You have made. I rejoice! Open my eyes to see opportunities to share Your joy . . .

JOYOUS LAUGHTER

*Then our mouth was filled with laughter, and our tongue
with shouts of joy. Psalm 126:2*

Did you know that laughter and joy are found together in Scripture more than once? While laughter is certainly not required of everyone who possesses the joy of Christ, it's no surprise that laughter may flow as a result of joy!

A glad heart makes a cheerful face. (Proverbs 15:13)

A warm smile and a little laughter can lighten and brighten our days. After all, we've got Jesus, so how can we help but rejoice in another day that He has made (Psalm 118:24)?

We were made in the image of God, and *He designed us* with the ability to express sheer joy—to smile, to laugh! While Scripture didn't record "Jesus laughed," it does say "Jesus wept" (John 11:35), and we know He experienced every emotion known to man. Just as sadness and sorrow may result in weeping, so gladness may result in joyous laughter.

A painting titled "Jesus Laughing" graces my living room wall as a constant reminder of Jesus' own joy. Contemporary American artist Ralph Kozak so beautifully portrayed Christ leaning His head back in joyous laughter.

In three brief years of ministry, Jesus taught multitudes and trained disciples. He healed the sick, lame, and demon-possessed. Jesus took every step with deliberate purpose on His journey to the cross. At the same time, Jesus had compassion on the multitudes and enjoyed fellowship with His closest companions.

Can you picture our Lord resting in the homes of His friends? During moments of respite from a rigorous ministry, Jesus reclined with friends over meals that included precious fellowship time. Perhaps gentle laughter ensued during their honest discourse.

Envision children scampering toward Jesus to be the first to sit near Him or crawl onto His lap. Joyous laughter likely erupted from His mouth, echoing their own (Mark 10:13–16).

Now picture Jesus following His resurrection as He makes breakfast for His disciples on the beach. (See John 21.) Unrecognized, He calls out to them in their boat, telling them to cast their nets on the other side. When a miraculous catch follows this command, Peter learns that it's the risen Lord who has called to them from shore. He jumps out immediately and swims for the beach to see his Savior. How do you think Jesus responds to the childlike excitement of His impetuous friend and follower? I envision His head tilted back as He laughs with joy!

This is the same Peter who attempted to walk on water with Jesus and was accomplishing the impossible until he looked down and fear seized him. The same Peter who cut off a guard's ear as Jesus was arrested. The same Peter who denied his Lord three times during Jesus' trial. Following this joyous moment with breakfast on the beach, Jesus reinstates Peter and asks him to feed His sheep because Jesus knows Peter's heart. He loves Peter despite his failings and takes great delight in him, the same way He loves and delights in you and me! Enough to die for him, just as He died for you and for me. Jesus endured the cross and rose again, all for the joy set before Him (Hebrews 12:2)—the joy of saving you and me.

May our mouths be filled with laughter and our tongue with shouts of joy. Joy in Jesus!

JOURNAL

What causes joyous laughter to erupt from you? Share specific memories and reasons for such laughter. Write about how it feels to know that Jesus delights in you.

PRAYER

Dear Jesus, thank You for the gifts of joy and laughter! Lead me to delight in others as You delight in me . . .

A JOYFUL NOISE

Make a joyful noise to the LORD, all the earth; break forth into joyous
song and sing praises! Psalm 98:4

One morning, a silly song played in my head as I washed the breakfast dishes. Suddenly, the words spilled out and I was singing aloud, "Oh,
Susanna, oh don't you cry for me, for I've come from Alabama with a banjo
on my knee!" I was belting out these words and slapping my knee when
my husband came around the corner. Cringing, Cory said, "Oh, Susanna?!
Really?!" He chuckled, shook his head, and kept walking.

I have this knack for connecting words to a song in unexpected ways,
even to me. Cory and I had just enjoyed a breakfast conversation that
included plans to visit our son in Alabama. The mere mention of the state
sparked the words and melody of this old tune. With thoughts of visiting
our son filling my mind, I didn't think to grumble over my dirty dishes.
Uninhibited, I broke forth in song concerning our Alabama adventure
that awaited!

Cory and I have been reading the Psalms during our morning devotions,
and he smiles as a verse parallels a line of a hymn, praise song, or VBS tune
because I suddenly *make a joyful noise* (often off-key). I mark music notes
beside them in my journaling Bible. To name a few:

He put a new song in my mouth, a song of praise to our
God. (Psalm 40:3)

Oh sing to the LORD a new song, for He has done marvelous
things! (Psalm 98:1)

Blessed be the LORD, the God of Israel, from everlasting to everlasting!
And let all the people say, "Amen!" Praise the LORD! (Psalm 106:48)

Some days it's easy to rejoice and sing! Other times, joy hasn't been as
obvious. God's Word tells me it's there, and I believe that's true: a fruit of

the Holy Spirit, joy is mine by faith. "I've got the joy, joy, joy, joy . . . down in my heart to stay." (Are you belting out these words with me now?!) So why can't I always see it? Why can't I always express Jesus' joy within me, "break[ing] forth into joyous song and sing[ing] praises?"

By God's grace, you and I can cling to the same faith for which Peter commended his fellow believers,

> Though you have not seen [Jesus], you love Him. Though you do not now see Him, you believe in Him and rejoice with joy that is inexpressible and filled with glory, obtaining the outcome of your faith, the salvation of your souls. (1 Peter 1:8–9)

Joy too deep for words, joy within us that God will use for His glory, the joy of our salvation by God's grace through faith in the One we cannot see!

JOURNAL

Choose a psalm and let the words be a balm for your soul. His joy is still yours, even on difficult days. What words make you break into song, whether from a familiar tune or a brand-new one?

PRAYER

Dear God, thank You for giving me every reason to make a joyful noise, to sing praises to You . . .

OOZING JOY

May the God of hope fill you with all joy and peace as you trust in Him, so that you may overflow with hope by the power of the Holy Spirit. Romans 15:13, NIV

A woman knocked on my front door the day after our church hosted a joy-themed women's retreat. She needed to share her heart with someone, and she blurted out in tears, "You women just ooze Jesus!" She went on to explain why the retreat impacted her so strongly. She'd hesitantly said yes to a friend's invitation and followed that friend through our doors for the first time. Throughout the event, she witnessed the joy of Jesus through the messages of several speakers. Each had vulnerably shared their hope in the promises of Christ as they spoke of their difficult journeys and God's work through them. He allowed this dear woman to see the joy of Jesus flowing—oozing—from them. It spilled onto her!

The Lord fills us to overflowing with a joy that only He can produce in us, by the Holy Spirit. *His joy is ours* despite circumstances; it exists even when happiness eludes us. Just as God's love has been poured into our hearts by the Holy Spirit (Romans 5:5), so, too, has the spiritual fruit of His joy (Galatians 5:22). And Jesus' joy is both contagious and abundant; it's caught by others as it overflows out of us and splashes onto them!

When the Samaritan woman sought to fill her water jar at a well, she encountered Jesus, who filled her with living water, the gift of faith. Overflowing with joy, the woman left her water jar behind and ran to her town, telling everyone about Jesus and beckoning them to come and see Him for themselves (John 4:29).

I believe we could say that this Samaritan woman oozed Jesus too. She couldn't contain her joy in Jesus for the gift she'd just received. The towns-people, who knew her difficult journey, witnessed her newfound joy in her message to them. Both contagious and overflowing, it apparently splashed onto them:

Many Samaritans from that town believed in [Jesus] because of the woman's testimony. (John 4:39)

Do you know that you ooze the joy of Jesus too? Filled with His joy as you trust in Him, your hope overflows by the Spirit's power—God working in you! Can you trust Him to use you, as He did the Samaritan woman—and as He used every speaker at our retreat—to do immeasurably more than you ask or think?

There is no limit to the joy that comes from Jesus because of the eternal hope we have in Him.

JOURNAL

When you read, "You . . . just ooze Jesus," who came to your mind? Describe that person's demeanor, words, or actions that made you think of her or him. Who gets to see you ooze Jesus?

PRAYER

Dear Jesus, I praise You for Your gift of faith! May I overflow with joy to a watching world . . .

GOOD NEWS OF GREAT JOY!

And the angel said to [the shepherds], "Fear not, for behold, I bring you good news of great joy that will be for all the people. For unto you is born this day in the city of David a Savior, who is Christ the Lord. And this will be a sign for you: you will find a baby wrapped in swaddling cloths and lying in a manger." Luke 2:10–12

In the quiet, dark hills above the village of Bethlehem, sleepy shepherds began their night watch like countless others in the fields with their flocks. Suddenly, light pierced through the darkness of the night sky and an angel of the Lord appeared to them in brilliant glory, announcing good news. The hope of the nations had come; the promised Christ was born! This good news, they were told, was "for all the people" and would give "great joy." Then appeared countless more angels—a heavenly host—all glorifying God at this momentous event, proclaiming peace between God and man, through the baby they would find lying in a manger.

On this joyous night, God spoke to the shepherds, announcing the greatest of news. And what did the shepherds do? Luke tells us that once the angels returned to heaven, the shepherds hurried to the manger. Envision them, eyes sparkling and hearts racing as they shouted to one another:

> "Let's go to Bethlehem and see this thing that has happened, which the Lord has told us about." So they hurried off and found Mary and Joseph, and the baby, who was lying in the manger. (Luke 2:15–16, NIV)

Like the shepherds, *we hear God speak to us*. We may not hear it proclaimed by His angels in the night sky, but we hear it just as clearly through His Word. We receive the Old Testament prophecies and learn of their perfect fulfillment in Christ. We read Luke's account and rejoice! The promised Christ has come; the Good News, fulfilled at the cross and the empty tomb, is proclaimed to us. Salvation is ours! When we hear it, do our eyes sparkle? Do our hearts race? Do we proclaim to one another, "Let's go"? The Lord is drawing us to Himself today, that we would come and worship Him now, as the shepherds did on the joyous night of His birth.

> When [the shepherds] had seen Him, they spread the word concerning what had been told them about this child, and all who heard it were amazed at what the shepherds said to them. . . . The shepherds returned, glorifying and praising God for all the things they had heard and seen, which were just as they had been told. (Luke 2:17–18, 20, NIV)

We recall the lowly shepherds' part in the nativity account today, mindful that the Lord chose these unlikely evangelists, just as He chooses you and me today, and He can do far more through our proclamations and praise than we can ask or imagine.

JOURNAL	PRAYER
"Let's go!" Hurry to Jesus . . . bring Him your praises right now, during your devotion time. What makes your eyes sparkle and causes your heart to race? Who will you take with you to spread the Word?	Holy Spirit, fill and strengthen me today, that I may share the good news of great joy that is, indeed, for all the people, even me . . .

JOY IN THE JOURNEY

You make known to me the path of life; in Your presence there is fullness of joy; at Your right hand are pleasures forevermore. Psalm 16:11

A common phrase like "joy in the journey" may roll off our tongues but with only a passing thought. Maybe you've said these words even if you weren't feeling particularly joyful because it seemed expected. Stop to consider the truth to this phrase, though. What if we lived by it instead of wishing away our day or looking for something on the horizon that has our attention?

What joy do we miss because we aren't looking for it? What do we overlook because we are focused on a future possibility (instead of a present reality)? Maybe we take today's joy for granted, failing to acknowledge the simple pleasures looking right back at us.

The psalmist nailed it when he proclaimed to God, "You will fill me with joy in Your presence." We are filled with His joy (yes, along today's particular journey) by His presence alone. He surrounds us, goes before and behind us, and has *His hand upon us* (Psalm 139:5). Not only does He "make known to [us] the path of life" in Jesus Christ, our Savior, but He walks that path with us every day, from now until eternity. He leads us in paths of righteousness (Psalm 23:3), providing light along the way by His Word (Psalm 119:105).

During a Hawaiian adventure, my family and I set out on a journey to the opposite side of the island with a specific destination (and reservations). While it was tempting to set our gaze solely on the GPS navigation keeping our course, if we had, we would have missed spectacular sights while passing through a handful of the Big Island's eight ecosystems. (An unplanned stop in the rainforest found us at a family-owned, branch-to-bar cacao farm, one of the day's highlights!) Oh, the joy in God's creative handiwork revealed before our eyes along the day's journey.

Have you wondered how and where God may provide you with immeasurably more along life's way, teaching you to enjoy the ride too? Joy in your journey may include unexpected interactions, quiet conversations, relationship growth, or new discoveries. Whether today's journey has you in the car or on foot, at work or play, at home or away . . . rejoice!

On our joy-filled journeys, every day and in every way, may we confess Christ as Lord of the journey as He directs our paths (Proverbs 3:6).

JOURNAL

Is there joy you've yet to recognize, as you focus on the present part of your journey? What reasons for joy stare back at you right now?

PRAYER

Lord of the journey, direct my path and open my eyes to see joy along the way . . .

IMMEASURABLY MORE
Gifts

CHOCOLATE CHIP OR OATMEAL RAISIN?

Oh, taste and see that the LORD is good! Blessed is the man who
takes refuge in Him! Psalm 34:8

*The day began, looking like a chocolate chip cookie . . . then one bite and
BAM! Oatmeal raisin.*

I don't remember where I first heard this silly phrase, but it spoke to
this chocolate-chip-cookie fanatic. Then it made me giggle. And then
it made me think. (You just nodded, giggled, or groaned because you can
relate on some level, right?)

Okay, so maybe it wasn't a literal cookie (or maybe it was), but we've all
had those days that began one way, then . . . BAM! We taste the unexpected.
Maybe the unwelcome. Maybe even the unpleasant.

What a relief to know that the Lord is good even on the not-so-tasty
days! You and I are blessed as we *take refuge in Him*, the One who provides
an immeasurable supply of His good gifts, beginning with His grace and
mercy for us in Christ, even as a day—or a season—hits us with an unexpected, unpleasant taste.

My friend Carol told me, "In either situation [life or cookies], we can set
ourselves up to accept positive or negative outcomes by staying in a state
of open-minded and open-hearted acceptance, praying that God will direct
our steps and be there at each step along the path. 'And we know that for
those who love God all things work together for good, for those who are
called according to His purpose' (Romans 8:28). Blessings come even from
unexpected, undesired events."

Another friend, Alicia, curbed my chocolate-chip thoughts as she shared her own: "I love oatmeal raisin too. . . . There have been so many times in my life that I thought I wanted the chocolate chip cookie only to make a decision or follow where God leads and realize that I have a yummy and delicious oatmeal raisin cookie instead. Sometimes God leads us down a different path than what we had planned, and it makes all the difference!"

Even if the "cookie" was exactly as you had expected, maybe your anticipation of that cookie outweighed the excitement that followed when you took that first bite. Or maybe the bite was even better. My friend Christie said it this way: "When eating [the cookie] or opening [the gift] is even more than what I anticipated . . . wow! What joy and amazement! Isn't that the way it is with God's gifts to us day after day? God is good way beyond our expectations! So, bring on the raisins, the chocolate, and whatever other goodies He has planned for us. To sit at [the] table with Jesus, face to face, is absolute joy! I do wait for that with anticipation, and it will be [immeasurably] more! Praise be to God!"

JOURNAL

When did an unexpected taste hit you unawares? Based on thoughts from my friends: (1) When have you seen blessings come in an unexpected package? (2) Share a time you thought you wanted one thing only to receive another, and you were surprised by its delicious "taste." (3) Write about one of God's gifts that exceeded your expectations.

PRAYER

Lord, You are good, as are all Your gifts! Thank You for the unexpected ones too . . .

SWEAT EQUITY AND ENERGY

*But thanks be to God, who . . . through us spreads the fragrance
of the knowledge of Him everywhere. For we are the aroma of
Christ to God. 2 Corinthians 2:14–15*

You're aware of your unique fingerprint. Maybe you've even studied voice analysis to know you possess an equally unique voice print. But did you know you have a one-of-a-kind sweat-print too? The complex chemical composition of every person's sweat is unique to them. It's true!

In Jesus' greatest commandment, He calls us to love God with all our heart, soul, mind, and strength (Mark 12:30). With all our strength. Might that include investing sweat equity as we serve? In our toughest tasks, we may even say they require blood, sweat, and tears.

Some days we do more than merely break a sweat. We are exhausted and uncomfortable following particularly hard labor, physical or otherwise. At the same time, maybe we're energized as we've sought to do the work and the will of God; as we've labored in the Lord, which is never in vain! (See 1 Corinthians 15:58.)

The energy we possess to serve God's purpose comes straight from the Lord too. As the apostle Paul proclaimed the good news of Christ, he said,

For this I toil, struggling with all His energy that He powerfully works within me. (Colossians 1:29)

Is our witness defined only by our actions, the kind that take physical energy and produce sweat? Like Paul, along with our actions, we use our words. Words that build up, encourage, and give grace to those who hear them (Ephesians 4:29). When I want to share important words, I break out in a cold sweat. How about you? As I stand before others to share Jesus, my heart races, beads of perspiration form on my forehead, and a trail of sweat trickles down my spine. Why? Adrenaline is flowing and my nerves are heightened, because, above all, I want to represent Jesus well.

Although I may stumble over my words and break a sweat, my Savior forgives me and guides me by the Spirit. Jesus literally shed His blood, sweat, and tears on the cross, trading His life for mine. Today, *He fills me with His grace* and provides me with all the energy I need as I live for Him and proclaim His name. In fact, He will do immeasurably more through my sweat equity than I can ask or imagine!

Maybe some days are sweatier than others. If someone tells you that you stink, just say thanks. The work you've done that produces your unique sweat-print is a sweet aroma to God in your sacrifice of service. You are loving people in Jesus' name as you serve—as you "spread the fragrance of the knowledge of Him" in response to all He's done for you. Yes, you have a unique sweat-print, and you are unique in every other way too. Your life story shared in your witness will be unique to you too.

JOURNAL

Share some of the ways you have recently invested sweat equity in your service at work, home, church, or elsewhere. What makes you break out in a cold sweat? Write your thoughts about the Lord's energy powerfully working in you, praising Him as you do.

PRAYER

God, thank You for spreading the sweet fragrance of Christ through me. Fill me with renewed energy as I serve in Your strength . . .

ON A MISSION!

For we are His workmanship, created in Christ Jesus for good works, which God prepared beforehand, that we should walk in them. Ephesians 2:10

Created in God's image (Genesis 1:27), designed with specific purpose, *you are called by God* with an assignment and a mission. Don't think so? Take another peek at today's theme verse above. God already knew, when He created you, what good works He would have for you to do. Your family heritage provides you with a unique background and story to share. Your life experiences have shaped and equipped you for the tasks ahead. Your relationships, opportunities, and circumstances are unique to you; they ready you for the road ahead too.

What do you automatically bring to the table for this assignment based on your cultural upbringing and past and present life experiences, all which God may utilize for another purpose?

Moses' Egyptian upbringing afforded him an understanding of the language and culture, preparing him for a future when he would stand in front of Pharaoh as a spokesman for God and His people. David's shepherding skills enabled him to defeat a giant with his weapon of choice, formerly used to protect his sheep. Paul drew upon his Roman citizenship to make his appeal to Rome, thus opening the door for the spread of the Gospel from prison.

Expect God to use some of your background, skills, and experiences as you answer His call, fulfill an assignment, or set out on a mission. Maybe that mission will include service within your own home and as connected to your church, or maybe it will take you far beyond your community. Which needs stir your desire to take action? What past or present experiences do you bring to the table? What gifts can you employ? What ignites your interest?

Maybe you have a wealth of experience with children and interact well with them. Perhaps you have a heart for the aging and homebound. Do you relate well with teens' unique challenges? Maybe you are multilingual. Are you experienced with spreadsheets and balancing budgets? Can you offer creative skills or marketing expertise? Maybe you've developed sound judgment and possess biblical insight.

Your mission may not require new or extraordinary skills or experience. But you can employ those you have already and utilize your uniqueness in service in God's kingdom on earth. As you set out, expect the Lord to do more through you than you can possibly project or even ponder, by the Spirit's power in you! You're on a mission.

JOURNAL

Write down several unique things about you, from your heritage to your upbringing to your life experiences, gifts, and training. Prayerfully consider how and where God will utilize your uniqueness.

PRAYER

Dear God, utilize everything about me for Your purpose; equip me to be on a mission for You always . . .

MAKE A BIG DEAL

Now there are varieties of gifts, but the same Spirit; and there
are varieties of service, but the same Lord; and there are varieties of activities, but it is the same God who empowers them all in
everyone. 1 Corinthians 12:4–6

Picture this: An athlete lifts his hands to the Lord following a victory. An artist places Christ at the center of her acceptance speech. A farmer gives thanks to God during an interview in the middle of his just-harvested field.

God blesses the athlete with skill and endurance. He provides the artist with creativity and inspiration. God gives the farmer fertile soil and good growth. (All this and more.) Why? So that His beloved people will showcase Him, the giver of every good gift (James 1:17), as their gifts bless others who receive the benefits.

The builder who recently remodeled a portion of our home is a godly man. As he interacts with subcontractors and laborers on the job, he speaks openly about his faith. He treats people with respect and practices a strong work ethic. When a project is complete, this man gives credit to each worker who did their part, and he gives glory to God, making much of Him.

Make a big deal about God; give Him the glory for every gift. Because He deserves it? Of course. Because a watching world wants to know where you get your gifts and who empowers you to use them? Absolutely. Magnify Him! Make a big deal about the One who gives you everything, including each talent you possess and every type of service or activity these talents lead you to do.

According to 1 Corinthians 12, there are varieties of gifts, service, and activities. Maybe you're an athlete, an artist, or a farmer; maybe your skill set has you performing, serving, or working in an entirely different way. In all activities, we serve the same God "who empowers them all in everyone" by the Spirit, who can do immeasurably more . . . through you!

The combination of what we say and all we do pretty much sums up our interactions with others and our impact upon them too:

Whoever speaks, as one who speaks oracles of God; whoever serves, as one who serves by the strength that God supplies—in order that in everything God may be glorified through Jesus Christ. (1 Peter 4:11)

He supplies all you need, and more, by His grace.

Thanks be to God for His inexpressible gift! (2 Corinthians 9:15)

JOURNAL

Write about one of your God-given gifts. What service or activity has (or could) this gift lead you to do? Through it, ask yourself: How could this glorify God and make much of Him?

PRAYER

Lord God, You empower me with every gift I have. May I make much of You in all I do . . .

AVERAGE OFFERINGS

*Whatever you do, in word or deed, do everything in
the name of the Lord Jesus, giving thanks to God the
Father through Him. Colossians 3:17*

I am average at a lot of things, like playing the piano, drawing, and mowing. Yes, mowing. My husband is talented in this area. He creates patterns, circles, and uniform lines. When he mows the lawn, we have a grassy work of art. When I mow, we have uneven rows in most places. It's okay that I'm not great at everything I attempt, even as I give my best effort (Colossians 3:23). But the perfectionist in me does not agree. I am impatient with my lack of excellence at several of my endeavors.

But my life—and therefore, my gifts—are placed in the hands of my Savior as I seek to do everything in His name. What does that mean? It means giving thanks to Him for each average gift and for the opportunity to use it for His glory. He may do more, make more, bless more than I am aware of as *He uses my average offerings* of these gifts. In fact, some of these average offerings have made an impact that I wouldn't have expected.

A particular piece of sheet music has stayed with me since my piano lesson days during childhood. My dad asks me to play this now-tattered arrangement of "How Great Thou Art" when he and my mom visit, because it's dear to him and evokes memories from my childhood. He has even asked me to play it during his funeral one day, when Jesus calls him home.

I love to draw, just for fun. And my grown son still tells me I'm an artist because I sketched his favorite "wild thing" for him, based on his favorite picture book when he was five. He has kept my precious drawing to this day.

Although my husband loves to mow, he's a busy guy and sometimes I step in, even surprising him with a mowed yard when he gets home. He doesn't mind the view, and he is grateful for my help.

Our God-given giftedness is not necessarily seen in a dream job,

Pinterest-worthy creations, or an enviable accomplishment. (These are not the "more" God has in mind.) Most often, our unique helpfulness happens through the everyday, average gifts we offer when we show up for others, manage daily tasks, and live out our vocations through simple acts of service.

Our talents don't have to be top-notch or professional quality to be used for good. Resting in Jesus, we offer up our gifts, sharing from our hearts and our hands. With great expectation, we can watch God multiply them for His glory, for others' benefit, and for our growth. (As my mowing skill improves, maybe someday my lines will actually be straight and I, too, will create a work of art!)

JOURNAL

Name several gifts at which you are average. How might God be using your everyday, average offerings to bless others and give Him glory?

PRAYER

Lord Jesus, thank You for every gift at which I excel and at which I'm average. Please use them for others' good and for Your glory . . .

CREATOR AND CREATED

Let all the earth fear the Lord; let all the inhabitants of the world
stand in awe of Him! For He spoke, and it came to be; He commanded,
and it stood firm. Psalm 33:8–9

I am in awe of God's creation! Aren't you? We are the pinnacle of His
handiwork, intricately designed, far more stunning than man's best creative
efforts. Even today's extravagant tools created via man-made technology
cannot compare with all of creation's complexity. From the expanse of the
universe to the tiniest molecule to the unique details that make up you and
me, *miraculous* describes all of it—every moment of life, every breath, every
piece of God's creation.

> He performs wonders that cannot be fathomed, miracles that cannot be
> counted. (Job 5:9, NIV)

God spoke and it was made. Every. Little. Detail. God formed us, chose
us by His grace, and saved us from our sin through Christ. Our humble
offerings are no match for His good gifts. Do we stand in awe? We should.
And by His grace, we do!

How can we respond to His life-giving gift of salvation for us? to His
magnificent creation around us? to His miraculous cell-level work within
us? The God of wonders is *continuously at work*, in countless ways and
via means that we may not yet know—to an extent beyond our biggest
imagination.

> You have multiplied, O Lord my God, Your wondrous deeds and Your
> thoughts toward us; none can compare with You! I will proclaim and
> tell of them, yet they are more than can be told. (Psalm 40:5)

His deeds and His thoughts toward me are so great and so many that
even as I proclaim and tell of them, I cannot possibly tell them all!

How precious to me are Your thoughts, O God! How vast is the sum of them! If I would count them, they are more than the sand. (Psalm 139:17–18)

His vast and loving thoughts toward us led the Father to send His Son, who completed the most wondrous deed in our place when He died for us and gave us new life in Him.

How can you and I respond in reverent fear and awe of God's gifts today? I'm pausing now to notice His creative work in me and around me. I feel the rhythmic movement of my heart as it beats. I see the evidence of a soft breeze by the movement of the trees nearby. I hear the sound of my own breath as I inhale sharply then exhale slowly. I rise from my writing chair to stand in awe of my Savior, who has gifted me with life forever in Christ and every other gift that flows from it.

JOURNAL

Pay attention to God's creative work in and around you, using different senses. Journal your observations. Then stand in awe, wherever you are, praising the Creator for the created, including you!

PRAYER

Lord of all creation, You spoke and it came to be! I praise You for Your thoughts and deeds for me . . .

GIFT GIVING

For the wages of sin is death, but the free gift of God is eternal life in Christ Jesus our Lord. Romans 6:23

Gift giving is one of my favorite hobbies. I study people, learn their interests, and keep an eye open for fitting gifts that will both delight and bless the recipients. Maybe my gift is something they need but cannot purchase for themselves. Or maybe it's a sweet treat to make them smile. To add to their experience, I nestle the gift in a tissue paper stuffed bag or wrap it in pretty paper and tie a ribbon around it. Christmas gift giving is my favorite because I'm reminded that the first and greatest gift was wrapped not in paper and bows but in swaddling cloths. And He is ultimately the reason for every gift I give.

We can admit that we are unworthy of any of God's gifts through the repentance worked in our hearts by the Holy Spirit. That same repentance causes us to *look to Jesus* as the one gift we need.

> And she gave birth to her firstborn son and wrapped Him in swaddling cloths and laid Him in a manger. (Luke 2:7)

God's gift was revealed to us in the flesh! Like a small child who has just unwrapped a favorite present, may our eyes grow wide—may we gasp in awe of the perfect gift we now behold!

God's gift through Jesus not only delights and blesses each recipient, it's a gift we cannot purchase for ourselves—or for anyone else, for that matter. All we can purchase by our sin is death. Amazingly, we receive instead God's free gift: eternal life in Christ!

The good news of forgiveness in Jesus is our gift of greatest need. And we can share it freely with all people. No matter who they are or what they have done, they, too, can receive the gift of His grace through faith and life forever in Him! We share this gift every time we say, "Jesus died for you!"

He is the giver of every good and perfect gift (James 1:17). From every sunrise to every tangible need; from every relationship to every opportunity, every good gift is ultimately from God's hand. His gifts *overflow* in our lives, thanks to the work of the Holy Spirit.

"You can't outgive God," my friend Karen Sue says. And it's true! He gives immeasurably more than you and I can hand out on all our most generous days combined! May every gift we give be an expression of His grace given to us in abundance and handed out through us just as generously. As we give gifts, we celebrate the greatest gift of all in our Savior.

JOURNAL

Do you enjoy gift giving? Write about favorite gifts you've given or received. Do you realize you are sharing a gift every time you share the Gospel? Journal your thoughts.

PRAYER

Dear Jesus, You are the perfect gift! Show me how and where I can share Your gifts . . .

GIFTED FOR GOD'S GLORY

Whatever you do, do all to the glory of God. 1 Corinthians 10:31

Cory has a pet squirrel he named Flicker. Okay, so Flicker is not his pet, but Cory likes to pretend that he is, largely for my benefit, so he can watch my eyes roll. Flicker entertains us as we gaze through the sunroom windows at our backyard tree where the squirrel makes his home. Flicker appears to be especially gifted, flying from one branch to another, scaling the top of the nearby fence, carrying corn cobs and other treasures while climbing. Just as the animals and birds in our tree give God glory by doing all that He created them to do, so it is with us!

God's creations carry out His good work: they simply do what they were created to do, fulfilling their God-given purpose. Maybe that sounds over-simplified as you contemplate God's plans for you and the use of your gifts in every purpose. So, let me ask you: What did God create you to do? The overarching answer: *Give Him glory!*

Now let's get specific: What can you do that gives Him glory? The pinnacle of His creation, you were crafted to love God and love others. Jesus said all of God's commandments could be summed up this way:

> You shall love the Lord your God with all your heart and with all your soul and with all your mind. This is the great and first commandment. And a second is like it: You shall love your neighbor as yourself. (Matthew 22:37–39)

Your giftedness, combined with your connections, personality, and proximity provide opportunities specific to you. What calls your name? Prayerfully follow the Lord's lead.

> As each has received a gift, use it to serve one another, as good stewards of God's varied grace: whoever speaks, as one who speaks oracles of God; whoever serves, as one who serves by the strength that

God supplies—in order that in everything God may be glorified through Jesus Christ. To Him belong glory and dominion forever and ever. Amen. (1 Peter 4:10–11)

By God's grace, you are gifted to serve others with words or actions or both. As a good steward of His gifts, how will you use them? In countless ways over time, to be sure. Speak His words of truth; serve in His strength; give Him the glory!

JOURNAL

Combine your giftedness with your connections, personality, and proximity to consider new and continued opportunities unique to you. What's one new way you will use a God-given gift and give Him the glory?

PRAYER

God, sometimes I complicate the good work You call me to do: love You and love others. Lead me to carry out Your purpose for me today . . .

CONTEXT MATTERS

For You formed my inward parts; You knitted me together in my mother's womb. I praise You, for I am fearfully and wonderfully made. Wonderful are Your works. Psalm 139:13–14

Context is everything. If I step into a conversation midstream, I'm likely to make a misguided guess about the bigger picture based on the limited words I heard. I might jump to incorrect conclusions or misinterpret one thing to mean another.

The same is true as I read Scripture. Take today's theme verses. Ideally, I'll read all of Psalm 139 to receive the fullness of King David's praises to God, his Creator. Even as I borrow a couple of verses for this devotion, I must be careful to interpret them well, since they're not being read within their larger context. Let's say I share only "I am fearfully and wonderfully made," and shout it aloud. While it's true, I may sound boastful in the presence of someone who is unfamiliar with the phrase or doesn't know the context or its origin. But these six words, combined within the phrases that precede and follow them, reveal fuller meaning together.

"I praise You" makes the following six-word phrase all the more meaningful, and it moves the focus to the Creator, who has so skillfully crafted us. Context from the previous verse teaches us even more about the intimate care that God has given to His creation, forming our inward parts, knitting us together in our mothers' wombs. The Lord's workmanship is "wonderful," David goes on to say. Every detail was fashioned with specific intent; we were "intricately woven" (v. 15). God knitted each of us together on purpose, *for a purpose* (fearfully and wonderfully, no less!).

Followers of Jesus, we come together in a community of faith; this is our context. The apostle Paul's inspired words relate this community to a human body. Christ is the Head of the church and we, God's chosen people in Christ, form the body together. Every member of the body is different, necessary, and complementary to the others:

For as in one body we have many members, and the members do not all have the same function, so we, though many, are one body in Christ, and individually members one of another. (Romans 12:4–5)

In this beautiful context, God will do immeasurably more than we can comprehend, as He works in every member for the good of the body and for His glory.

Wonderful are His works, indeed! We need one another. One member, removed from the context of the body, would not be able to best serve His unique purpose because, by the body's design, each part is dependent upon the others. As all members work together, according to their wonderful design, the Body of Christ grows and "builds itself up in love" (Ephesians 4:15–16). Context matters.

JOURNAL

Recall a time when you accidentally took words out of context. Was the meaning confused, incomplete? What happens when a Christian is removed from her context of community? Share your thoughts.

PRAYER

Dear God, I praise You for creating me and placing me in the context of community—the Body of Christ . . .

DEAR YOUNGER ME

Having gifts that differ according to the grace given to us, let us use them. Romans 12:6

I sat on the swing in our big backyard, lost in creative thought, singing and speaking aloud to myself. I was working on lyrics for a love song. At a tender age of ten, I was certain "Love Is like a Swing" would become a greatest hit. The nearest neighbor was miles away from our farm, so I belted out my new melody with confidence, imagining an audience all around me. Later, I learned the farmhouse windows were open when my mom asked, "Were you singing outside, Debbie?" She thought it was nice. I panicked, then lied. I insisted that I'd just been talking to myself. Why was I embarrassed by my voice, too timid to admit my singing to my own mother? I'd love to tell ten-year-old me that I don't have to be embarrassed by my singing voice.

> Dear Younger Me,
>
> Sing out loud, whether someone hears you or not. It's okay either way because God will use your timidity to give you future empathy for your own children's hesitations.
>
> Your gifts and abilities matter, even if they're different than others' or unrecognizable to some.
>
> Resist comparison of your gifts to others'. Instead, recognize their complementary nature.
>
> Just you wait! You won't believe all the things God is going to do through you. He is working in you already, producing gifts and talents He will use, providing future opportunities to grow in them and open doors through which you will express them.
>
> He who fashioned your heart sees all that you do (Psalm 33:15). He forgives you in Christ for every misstep . . . and

you should know this too: "The LORD your God is in your midst, a mighty one who will save; He will rejoice over you with gladness; He will quiet you by His love; He will exult over you with loud singing" (Zephaniah 3:17).

Now, I see so many places and pieces of my younger years where God was working.

Now, I can recount some of the ways He used what I was learning then.

Now, I see where He did *immeasurably more* through me than I could have hoped or envisioned in my younger years. That doesn't always mean it's a great big, recognizable thing (according to the world, anyway), but it matters to God and to the person who was impacted by my God-given gifts.

Are you a creative planner or a number cruncher? A hand holder or a humble teacher? Give God the glory, acknowledging that it's Christ's gift in you (Ephesians 4:7), by His grace, for the good of others.

Dear Younger Me, maybe the love of God is a little like a swing, enabling you to move in ways you couldn't on your own and giving you a secure place to sit when you need to be still.

JOURNAL

Read Romans 12:6–8 and write the variety of gifts mentioned there. Under which categories do your gifts fall, and how do you use them? What would you say to your younger self regarding your gifts?

PRAYER

Dear Lord God, thank You for enabling me to see that You were using me when I was young, just as You use me now, for Your glory . . .

IMMEASURABLY MORE

Rest

SURROUND SOUND

Mary . . . sat at the Lord's feet and listened to His teaching. But Martha was distracted with much serving. Luke 10:39–40

A cacophony of sound swirls around me. My inbox pings with every new piece of mail. The doorbell rings, announcing another delivery. My phone buzzes as the texts pile up. The news broadcasts another alert. Most days, I'm distracted by sensory overload. A constant stream of messages flows past me, calling out to me, beckoning me to go! Do! Run!

Could one sound dominate above the noise of all the others when we're in desperate need of rest? I journaled this question as I lay on Waikiki's white sand beach, pen in hand. Enjoying a restful afternoon with me, my husband remarked that the pounding surf drowned out other vacationers' voices and created an oddly tranquil atmosphere, even though we were surrounded by people. The powerful roar of water was, at the same time, peaceful. The ocean's waves, when they kissed the shore, created a calming surround sound.

I want the *Lord's voice* to be the one I hear above all others, though it may come to me as a whisper (see 1 Kings 19:11–12) as His Word speaks tenderly to my heart. Then again, He may speak with the volume of a wave kissing the shore, as the Word convicts me in my sin, then reassures me of my salvation in Christ.

Can you imagine the cacophony of sounds that surrounded Jesus throughout His ministry? Crowds pressed in and people cried out from every direction . . . and Jesus had compassion for all. He also stepped away for rest, and that included meals in the home of friends. On one such occasion, He was dining in Bethany (Luke 10:38–42) at the home of siblings Mary, Martha, and Lazarus. Martha was distracted with the "sounds" of serving her guests, but Mary sat at Jesus' feet. She listened to the Lord's teaching, and as Jesus reminded Martha later, Mary had chosen the one thing necessary.

Only with the Lord's help can we choose the one thing necessary. (Thank You, Jesus!) How can we surround ourselves with the sound of the Savior's voice? Envision His embrace; remember that His presence and protection truly do surround you. Tune in to God's Word; focus on the One who walks with you even while other voices beckon and duty calls.

As powerfully as the surf pounds, far greater is His power by the Spirit to provide focus for us, that we may sit at His feet and receive rest in Him. Knowing His hand is always upon us, we find real rest, even as we face multiple demands and distractions within a given day.

(By the way, He leads me to rest with Him, away from those distracting noises, when I turn off the TV, close my computer, silence my phone, and step away from the door.)

JOURNAL

What sounds surround you? What will help you tune in to God's voice? A daily verse app? Christian music? Bible study with a faithful friend? What works for you? Try something new.

PRAYER

Dear God, surround me with the sound of Your voice . . . lead me to sit at Your feet . . .

PEACEFUL SLEEP

*In peace I will both lie down and sleep; for You alone, O Lord,
make me dwell in safety. Psalm 4:8*

Our son struggled nightly with anxious thoughts. When his body began to rest, his mind began to stir from the stress of the day. Part of our tuck-in routine included me singing "I Love You, Lord" while stroking his hair or scratching his back. After we'd talked through a few of the day's events and prayed over them together, his heartbeat would slow to a restful pace as his thoughts returned to a peaceful place. Our son knew he was safe and sound, tucked not only into bed but also into the Savior's care.

I've struggled with similar anxious thoughts and stress. They threaten to keep me awake too. While my heart races, I repeat from memory, "Do not be anxious about anything" (Philippians 4:6). I remember that the Lord doesn't say this to scold me, but to remind me to *turn to Him* when anxious thoughts creep in, threatening my would-be peaceful sleep.

> Do not be anxious about anything, but in everything by prayer and supplication with thanksgiving let your requests be made known to God. And the peace of God, which surpasses all understanding, will guard your hearts and your minds in Christ Jesus. (Philippians 4:6–7)

As I've asked God to take my anxious thoughts from me, I have named ways in which I'm thankful; I've recalled His past provision and constant care. In many ways, I talk with God as my son talked with me during tuck-in time. My Lord sings over me (Zephaniah 3:17), my heart returns to a restful pace, and I sleep in peace, "For You alone, O Lord, make me dwell in safety."

Anxiety is real, and as you and I face every stress and struggle in this sin-ridden world, we receive from the Lord an action plan for rest, found in Philippians 4. What can we do when our minds stir from the stressors of the day? Securely tucked and covered in God's grace, we can pray about everything with an attitude of thanksgiving, trusting Him to guard us with a peace so great that it surpasses our understanding.

When I go to bed and anxious thoughts swirl, singing Scripture sets my soul at rest. I remember all the ways God was faithful throughout the day, and I praise Him with song that settles me:

By day the LORD commands His steadfast love, and at night His song is with me, a prayer to the God of my life. (Psalm 42:8)

JOURNAL

Share a song or a prayer that you could sing or speak when anxious thoughts stir from the stressors of your day. Adopt a verse or two that you may say. Recall a piece of God's past provision and give thanks.

PRAYER

Dear Lord God, thank You for providing all I need. Remove my anxious thoughts and replace them with Your peace . . .

THE NEXT RIGHT THING

Blessed is the man who trusts in the Lord, whose
trust is the Lord. Jeremiah 17:7

Pause in the middle of your day to look up and lift your hands in praise. Rejoice that this is another day the Lord has made, and you are here for it! (Bring it on!) Your times are in God's hands (Psalm 31:15) just as He holds you in His hand (Psalm 139:10). You can rest, assured that He has you in His grip. He is worthy of your complete trust. In fact, He *is* your trust. You don't have to overthink each step, just do the next right thing.

Sometimes it's difficult to simply do the next right thing, a popular directive these days. I interpret it to mean following the Lord's lead instead of attempting to forge a trail myself, as though I'm on my own or in charge. It means taking the next single step. And although I don't know what the future holds, I know who holds the future . . . and me.

How will we know if (fill in the blank) is the next right thing? We can ask ourselves: *Will it give glory to God? Does it align with God's truth revealed for us in the Bible? Might others benefit from it?* If we can give an affirmative answer to these questions, then we can move forward with confidence as we seek to do right versus wrong, to do right by our neighbor, and to do the Next. Right. Thing.

However, let us not attempt this thing (or anything, for that matter) in our own strength as though we're pulling a proverbial rope, hoping God will help if we run out. This attempt isn't just exhausting, it's fruitless! We can let go of the rope and *trust in the Lord* who makes our steps firm. Even if we should stumble, we are in His grip, and we will not fall:

The Lord makes firm the steps of the one who delights in Him; though he may stumble, he will not fall, for the Lord upholds him with His hand. (Psalm 37:23–24, NIV)

Jesus did all the work to reconcile us to God; He is the strength in us today too. How did we receive Christ? By grace through His gift of faith, which He poured out at our Baptism. How are we called to live in Christ each day? Again, by grace through faith. To God be the glory!

> Therefore, as you received Christ Jesus the Lord, so walk in Him, rooted and built up in Him and established in the faith. (Colossians 2:6–7)

We take the next step with Him right beside us and working in us, doing immeasurably more through each next step than we can ask or imagine. May we trust Him today as we show up and seek direction for each step. May we keep asking Jesus to help us do the next right thing . . . and then the next . . .

JOURNAL

Read Proverbs 3:5–6 and write it here. How does trusting the Lord relate to rest and doing the next right thing?

PRAYER

Dear Jesus, lead the way and hold my hand; help me do the next right thing . . .

JESUS & ME

Oh, how abundant is Your goodness, which You have stored up for those who fear You and worked for those who take refuge in You, in the sight of the children of mankind! Psalm 31:19

I have a Jesus-and-me space, and it calls my name. My space may not always be in the same place; it may move according to the season and my mood, but it's almost always a space in my home where I meet God in His Word for time together. We can be found on the back patio on sunny summer mornings or in the sun room on chillier autumn days. We meet in the living room in the winter, curled up in my cozy, overstuffed chair. And we chat in the kitchen throughout every season, pulled up to the table next to a hot cup.

I keep a basket in my space, and I fill it with a handful of helpful tools: my Bible (of course!), a devotional, a journal, a pen, and a Bible study or two. The basket may also contain colored pencils, note cards, and dark chocolate, for good measure. While all these tools are great, ultimately, my space is about Jesus meeting me in His Word as I respond to Him and pray. And in this quiet time, I receive daily rest and refuge in Him.

I like to set a scheduled time, but flexibility for Jesus and me is essential too, since schedules change and every day is different, to some extent. The best part about flexibility? *Jesus is always available.* I don't have to wonder or wait to see if He will meet with me.

Something I've come to expect every time we meet is His work in me, by the power of the Holy Spirit through the living, active Word. I ask God to change me until my will aligns with His, and I trust His will to be done (Matthew 6:10) across all my requests. So, I humbly lay them at His feet, knowing God's ways are higher and better than mine (Isaiah 55:8–9).

Immeasurably more than we can ask is the Lord's *good* that He has in store for us—that He has "stored up" for us—when we rest with Jesus in His

Word. There, we see just how good God is! Jesus' completed work for us at the cross provides forgiveness and eternal life. And He works His abundant goodness in us, creating change and producing growth. He brings transformation by the Holy Spirit. Amazing things happen when we are on our knees or seated at Jesus' feet.

Confident of this, I return to the refuge of my Jesus-and-me space. You can create or return to yours too, wherever that may be. His abundant goodness is for you and me.

JOURNAL

Describe the space(s) where you meet with Jesus. What helpful tools do you use? When do you like to meet? The quiet of the early morning? Just before bed? Another time? Rest in His embrace, whatever the space.

PRAYER

Jesus, lead me to the daily rest I find in You, no matter where I am or what else my day holds. Change me. Make me more like You . . .

I WILL GIVE YOU REST

[Jesus said,] "Come to Me, all who labor and are heavy laden, and I will give you rest. Take My yoke upon you, and learn from Me, for I am gentle and lowly in heart, and you will find rest for your souls. For My yoke is easy, and My burden is light." Matthew 11:28–30

I'm often striving toward something. I labor to lose weight and make every effort to eat healthy meals; I attempt new projects and work on old ones; I do my best to start a good habit and strive to kick a bad one. The world tells us to be a better version of ourselves. So, we set goals. They sound good . . . and, often, they are. But we may set an unrealistic, unattainable goal, only to feel like a failure when we cannot or do not follow through. Or what if our goal simply doesn't fall in line with God's greater plan?

The heart of man plans his way, but the Lord establishes his steps. (Proverbs 16:9)

I don't know about you, but I'm tired of trying so hard.

Jesus speaks into our weary, heavy-laden days with His offer of rest. Turning away from our goal-oriented lives, we rest in His completed work for us at the cross and the empty tomb. There, we find rest for our souls—for today and for eternity. Whatever goals we may strive for, salvation is not one of them!

But what about our daily labors? Sometimes we behave as though we have to prove ourselves worthy to the rest of the world. "Look over here! I'm trying . . . and I'm a better version of myself today than I was yesterday!" Jesus has answers for that too. He forgives us for our faulty attempts to prove our worth, and He walks with us daily. Envision a full-grown oxen yoked—connected—with a yearling as they work side by side. Jesus takes the weight of our load; we follow His lead, *leaning into His strength*, and we learn every step of the way. His yoke is easy; His burden is light.

Whatever your goals, look and listen to the Lord first. Lean on Jesus, and follow His lead. He may surprise you with all that He has in store. And you can rest, assured that He will never fail you, even as you fear the possibility of your own failure.

We often think that striving toward a new goal means making a 180-degree change. But did you know that even a one-degree shift changes our trajectory and the outcome? It's true! Our small steps, guided by our Savior, may provide great blessings, as He does immeasurably more through our minor attempts than we can imagine, by His power at work within us.

Every day we get a reset, a chance to start anew, a fresh new beginning thanks to Jesus!

The steadfast love of the LORD never ceases; His mercies never come to an end; they are new every morning; great is Your faithfulness. (Lamentations 3:22–23)

Rest in this truth too.

JOURNAL

Prayerfully consider some goals you'd like to attempt, following the Lord's lead. Then consider His ability to use even a one-degree shift for immeasurably more than you can imagine, as the Spirit works in and through you.

PRAYER

Lord Jesus, thank You for the rest You offer me today and for eternity. Lead me as I lean into Your strength . . .

SUPERHERO

But He said to me, "My grace is sufficient for you, for My power
is made perfect in weakness." Therefore I will boast all the
more gladly of my weaknesses, so that the power of Christ may
rest upon me. 2 Corinthians 12:9

If you could choose a superhuman quality, what would it be? Would you
be able to scale tall buildings? Travel through time? Defy gravity? Fly?

In my mind, I can still feel the worn corners of my baby blanket tied
together around my shoulders, creating a makeshift cape. I'd stand atop the
wide armrest of our sofa, extend my arms, and jump while flapping furi-
ously. A few times I was certain I'd flown for a millisecond or two. *Sigh.* I was
never able to fly. I guess I'm not superhuman. Just human.

I cannot drape myself in some kind of superhero cape and expect to
magnify my own might. You and I can't conquer our sin, our enemy, or the
world on our own; we couldn't if we tried. *Jesus conquered all* in one fell
swoop! In our weakness, may we be even more mindful of the incompre-
hensible, unlimited power that rests upon us, by His all-sufficient grace.
Our strength comes from our Savior; our might is in our Maker.

Jesus is the hero in every one of our stories. He is the epitome of good,
who fights every evil and secures the final victory on our behalf. Romans 8
reads as the victorious finale of a superhero story:

Who shall separate us from the love of Christ? Shall tribulation, or
distress, or persecution, or famine, or nakedness, or danger, or
sword? . . . No, in all these things we are more than conquerors
through Him who loved us. For I am sure that neither death nor life,
nor angels nor rulers, nor things present nor things to come, nor
powers, nor height nor depth, nor anything else in all creation, will
be able to separate us from the love of God in Christ Jesus our Lord.
(Romans 8:35, 37–39)

Our hero holds the victory, so that in Him, we are called conquerors too.

- ♥ In our lack, we find His plenty.
- ♥ In our frailty, we obtain His strength.
- ♥ In our shortcomings, we rest in His abundance.
- ♥ In our failures, we are given His victory.
- ♥ In our inability, we receive His finished work for us!

No, you cannot be superhuman, but you can just be yourself. And who is that? A dearly loved child of God (1 John 3:1), forgiven and chosen in Christ, your Savior. Rest in His saving grace, confident that He who began a good work in you will carry it to completion on the day of Jesus' return (Philippians 1:6).

Yes, you and I seek to grow and improve every day, but striving for superhero status is not the answer. Lean on your true superhero who makes you not just better, but mature and complete, lacking nothing (James 1:4), covered in His perfect status alone.

JOURNAL

What superhuman quality would you choose? Why? Where have you witnessed your Savior's power in your weakness, enabling you to rest in Him? Which of the bulleted qualities in this devotion stood out to you especially well today? Why?

PRAYER

Jesus, Your power rests upon me; in You I find rest. You truly are my hero . . .

CAST YOUR BURDENS

Cast your burden on the Lord, and He will sustain you; He will never permit the righteous to be moved. Psalm 55:22

Greater than what I am going through is who I am becoming in Christ.

Read that again, then let me ask you this: What are going through in this season of life? this year? this day? Maybe you're literally going through memories and sorting through belongings as you pack to move. Or perhaps you're going through some big life changes with exciting opportunities on the horizon. Maybe you're going through a slow season, and you're stuck in the doldrums. Or maybe you're going through a hard season that includes relationship difficulties, nagging worries, or ongoing illness.

Whatever you're going through, God knows your thoughts, expectations, and fears. He sees your physical and relational concerns. He is with you amid every circumstance. He understands that you may be anything but restful in this season or on this day for all you're going through!

In His Word, God calls us to *trust Him with our whole heart* (Proverbs 3:5), and He enables us to do it! So cast your burdens on the Lord and rest in Him as you trust Him to sustain you, whatever comes to pass. Trust Him to strengthen your faith, that you may not be moved. Trust Him to provide for you, even if you're slow to recognize His provision when it looks different than you expected.

Let's do some casting. Whether you've ever gone fishing or not, will you indulge me by picking up your imaginary rod and reel? Raise your arm and fling your wrist forward. Do you see the line you just cast, waaaay out there on the water? Now envision casting your burdens and anxieties onto the Lord in the same manner.

[Cast] all your anxieties on Him, because He cares for you. (1 Peter 5:7)

What will you reel in?

Cast your burden of loneliness. Reel in God's provision through a new coworker or friend.

Cast your burden of worry. Reel in the peace He provides during worship and the encouragement He gives through people in the pew near you.

Cast your burden of indecision. Reel in wisdom through His Word and the godly counsel of others.

Immeasurably greater than all you're going through is who you are becoming in Christ. Trust His work in you by the power of the Spirit. He has a purpose. He will use whatever you're going through for far more than you can imagine, for good and for His glory. Who is He making you to be as a result? More like Jesus (2 Corinthians 3:18).

JOURNAL

Spend some time writing what you're going through, whether exciting, new, difficult, or otherwise. Have you thought about who you are becoming in the process? Do some casting today, whatever your burden may be.

PRAYER

Dear Lord Jesus, as I cast my burdens on You, I trust You to reel in all I need . . .

TAKE A BREAK!

And [Jesus] said to them, "Come away by yourselves to a desolate place and rest a while." For many were coming and going, and they had no leisure even to eat. Mark 6:31

I've run a few races, from 5ks to half marathons, and I've learned that the longer the race, the more breaks I need to take. A quick water break is essential when I'm parched; I catch my breath and rehydrate for the stamina to go the distance—to cross the finish line on my feet. At the end of any long run, extended rest is necessary for muscle recovery and to recuperate from physical fatigue.

Much of our journey is marked by marathon-length commitments. If we leave the starting line at a sprint, we'll fall flat on our face long before the finish line. Sustainability for the long road ahead requires a manageable pace balanced with regular breaks.

Jesus sent out His twelve apostles on a task of marathon proportions, giving them authority and power to teach, cast out demons, and heal the sick (Mark 6:7, 12–13). People came to the apostles constantly. The men had been so busy, they had no time to take a break, not even for a meal. When the apostles returned to Jesus and reported all they'd done in His name (v. 30), He knew their tired state. Ever mindful of His followers' needs, Jesus told them, "Come away by yourselves to a desolate place and rest a while." Jesus encouraged physical rest. He knew His disciples needed it.

The rigors of regular work—whether in ministry, at the office, on the assembly line, in the classroom, or at the farm—necessitate rest. God is glorified through your work and in your rest. He can do immeasurably more than you ask or think as *the Spirit works in you*, whatever you do!

You were created for a rhythm that includes motion and stillness, movement and rest. If you've battled burnout or even exhaustion, have you noticed a difference after you finally stop to catch your breath? Do you see an improvement in your stamina and your wellness when you make regular pit stops along the way?

It is in vain that you rise up early and go late to rest, eating the bread of anxious toil; for He gives to His beloved sleep. (Psalm 127:2)

Commit your cares to Him; He longs to give you rest.

Resting from work looks different depending on the kind of work you do. Rest might involve something very active if your daily work is sedentary. On the other hand, if work is physically rigorous, your rest may include a nap or a quiet activity. Just remember, the rest you can receive in Christ is incomparably better than mountain hikes, ocean cruises, or spa days. Any rest regimen without Christ is incomplete; it's simply less than we need. So . . . curl up in God's Word; learn something new about your faith; pray and praise Him as you explore the Bible.

Whether you are running a marathon or running with the Good News of Jesus, take intentional breaks to rest along life's way.

JOURNAL

Write about a recent break you have taken: What did you do and how did it help you? Plan a day of rest. What will your day include? Reflection? Journaling? Walk-and-talk time with the Lord?

PRAYER

Dear Jesus, You know when and why I need to take a break. Thank You for the rest I find with You and in You . . .

HE KEEPS YOU . . .
AND THEM TOO

The LORD will keep your going out and your coming in from this time
forth and forevermore. Psalm 121:8

I miss my grown-up kids every day. Whether I will see them in a week or wonder when our next time together will be, I have them on my heart. I'll admit, I worry about them too. My mind wanders to the days when they were under my roof. I rested so well when they were tucked in each night, safe within my care. Years ago, when I had shared my parenting worries, seasoned parents remarked to me, "At least they're under your roof and you know they're safe!" Now I understand what they meant!

Our children are scattered across the country now, and I'm accustomed to their autonomy. While I wish we were closer geographically, I trust that the One who connects us has all our backs continuously. When my children are on my heart, I pray with wonder at our omnipresent God, whose protection covers us wherever we are. He knows their thoughts and needs, just as He knows mine. I rest in these truths as I rest in the One who "will keep [their] going out and [their] coming in" today, tonight, tomorrow . . . and forever. When worries rise, I lift them to the Lord. I lay every care at His feet, by His grace, and I envision His watchfulness over each of them as I pray.

Psalm 121 is "A Song of Ascents." The faithful would sing this on their way to Jerusalem as they ascended to the city on a hill. While they made their way, all around them were pagan shrines with idols standing tall on the hills. But where would their help come from? Not from idols, but from the Lord, Creator and Savior of all, whom they would worship when they arrived.

Pray this psalm today—over your loved ones and over yourself:

I lift up my eyes to the hills. From where does my help come? My help comes from the LORD, who made heaven and earth. He will not let your foot be moved; He who keeps you will not slumber. Behold, He who keeps Israel will neither slumber nor sleep. The Lord is your keeper; the Lord is your shade on your right hand. The sun shall not strike you by day, nor the moon by night. The Lord will keep you from all evil; He will keep your life. The Lord will keep your going out and your coming in from this time forth and forevermore. (Psalm 121)

Pray this psalm over your children, your parents, or any family members God has placed on your heart. *With His help*, you can release your worry and entrust them to His care. Personalize these words as you make your way through each day. Lift your eyes to Jesus, who keeps you, even as He keeps your loved ones, wherever they may be. You can rest well, knowing that He never sleeps—even as you sleep under separate roofs. Trust your keeper to do immeasurably more through your humble prayers than you may ever know.

JOURNAL

Rest in the Lord's omnipresence. He is with your family members too. Circle every "keep(s)" in Psalm 121 above. What truth will you pray for your loved ones who aren't presently with you?

PRAYER

Dear God, my help comes from You! Thank You for keeping my loved ones and me in Your constant care . . .

HE HOLDS YOUR HAND

Nevertheless, I am continually with You; You hold my right hand. You guide me with Your counsel, and afterward You will receive me to glory. Psalm 73:23–24

Why does evil so often appear to have the upper hand? In our fallen world, we witness depravity, hate, and violence. Verbal attacks run rampant under the guise of good; decisions are made that defy the authority of God's Word. None of this is unique to our time in history either. Asaph, the writer of Psalm 73, lamented similarly, concerning the evil of his day. He cried out, "[The wicked] are not in trouble as others are; they are not stricken like the rest of mankind. Therefore pride is their necklace; violence covers them as a garment. . . . They set their mouths against the heavens, and their tongue struts through the earth" (vv. 5–6, 9). Then as now, it may seem that those opposed to God are prospering and victorious, and we become distraught, like Asaph, over the apparent upper hand of the unfaithful. So, it may be tempting to become bitter or envious, even to turn our gaze to them. Asaph confessed, "My feet had almost stumbled, my steps had nearly slipped. For I was envious of the arrogant when I saw the prosperity of the wicked" (vv. 2–3).

Because we see evil flagrantly displayed, we may begin to think that God doesn't know or care or control all things, as those who've followed the ways of the wicked claim: "They say, 'How can God know? Is there knowledge in the Most High?'" (v. 11).

What did Asaph do in his anguish when he could not understand? He went into the sanctuary of God and received discernment (vv. 16–17). Always and ultimately, God prevails!

Asaph's lament turned to praise for all that He knew to be true:

Nevertheless, I am continually with You; You hold my right hand. You guide me with Your counsel, and afterward You will receive me to glory.

Whom have I in heaven but You? And there is nothing on earth that I desire besides You. My flesh and my heart may fail, but God is the strength of my heart and my portion forever. For behold, those who are far from You shall perish; You put an end to everyone who is unfaithful to You. But for me it is good to be near God; I have made the Lord GOD my refuge, that I may tell of all Your works. (Psalm 73:23–28)

We go to the sanctuary of God's Word to receive discernment. In these six verses, we praise Him with Asaph because *the Lord also holds our hands*. Throughout this life, He guides and gives us counsel by His Word, and at the day of Christ's return, He will receive us to glory! Everything this world offers pales in comparison to all that awaits us in heaven. In our sin, we were once far from God, but in Christ we are forgiven and brought near, by His grace. He is our portion forever. In our weakness, He is strong. We find rest in the One who is our refuge, and we shout His praises to the world!

JOURNAL

What makes you distraught? Which of Asaph's praises are especially comforting to you today? (He holds your hand . . . He guides you . . . He is your strength . . . Another?) Find comfort in Romans 8:31–32 too; write the verses here:

PRAYER

Lord God, You prevail! And You hold my hand. I rest in You . . .

IMMEASURABLY MORE
Life

LIFE WITH ONE ANOTHER

May the God of endurance and encouragement grant you to live in
such harmony with one another, in accord with Christ Jesus, that
together you may with one voice glorify the God and Father of our
Lord Jesus Christ. Romans 15:5–6

"Doing life together" is a catchphrase commonly used today, and I like
it! I'm so glad God created us for community; I cannot imagine "doing life"
without the close connections, support, and mutual encouragement we
find in one another. Did you know that the New Testament has more than
thirty-five "one another" commands and some appear multiple times? Love
one another (Romans 12:10), serve one another (Galatians 5:13), comfort and
agree with one another (2 Corinthians 13:11) are a few, to start.

Clearly, we need one another, and this is according to God's design. But
when am I merely selective or self-serving with my connections? I meet
for coffee with friends and collaborate over ministry projects with like-
minded leaders. I spend time shopping with easygoing girlfriends, I enjoy
travel time with family, and I love meal time with my husband . . . and a few
close friends too. Much of my time is spent with those who are part of my
friend group, with those who provide mutual affirmation. I'm relaxed when
I spend time with those who "get" me (and vice versa). However, I fear letting some people get too close to me when they're demanding, negative, or
different than me, when time with them means hard conversations. Maybe
they challenge me in a way that makes me test my status quo. Maybe time
together hurts because they point out truth that I don't want to admit or
see. Ouch! I am convicted by my limited care for others, and I take it to

the Lord in prayer. Thanks be to God for His amazing grace and forgiveness in Christ.

Too many times to count, I have been humbled as I get to know someone better. The Lord has graciously softened my heart to see this other person more clearly. Often my first impression of this person was wrong, my worries were unfounded, or the words I needed to hear for my growth or humility come from that very person. We may not become best friends, but I do not want to hide from fellow believers whom I've deemed difficult. I don't wish to avoid hard conversations with them either, because I sure don't want to miss the amazing outcomes God may produce through shared time and experience as we "do life together." Yes, you and I can expect our Savior to do far more abundantly than all we ask or think, as *He works in us* while we serve, side by side, with one another.

Jesus didn't say this life with others would be easy, but the one who provides endurance and encouragement will enable us to live in harmony, according to His will, so that together we give Him glory (Romans 15:5–6)! Ahh! The outcome is worth every effort when it is guided by God's grace.

JOURNAL

Write about several people you enjoy doing life with. How does each of them provide support, share affirmation, collaborate, or rest with you? Look up a few "one another" verses and prayerfully consider spending intentional time in this way with someone new.

PRAYER

Dear God, lead me to live in harmony and fellowship with everyone around me as we "do life together," loving one another . . .

RUNNING IN CIRCLES

Let us also lay aside every weight, and sin which clings so closely, and let us run with endurance the race that is set before us, looking to Jesus, the founder and perfecter of our faith. Hebrews 12:1–2

I walk around . . . and around . . . and around the practice track behind my house, and it looks like I'm going—and getting—nowhere! While I love the convenience and cushioned surface this track affords me as I exercise, I'm literally not getting anywhere new.

Any analogy of running or racing in circles is so fitting as I consider the hurry, hurry, hurry that gets me nowhere new in life. If I'm honest, I often get caught in an endless cycle of striving to get ahead. *Ahead of what?* Maybe the purpose behind people's striving varies. Sometimes we strive for financial gain; other times it's for increased social media influence. Maybe it's the upward spread of sales or the increased attention or attraction of others. Even good goals can become self-focused. When might our striving become solely about achieving personal victory?

I know that my worth is not measured in earthly pursuits. I confess the sin that "clings so closely," and I ask the Lord first for His grace—and receive it *freely in Christ*. Then I ask for God's strength to stop running in competitive circles, but to run an infinitely better race that's already marked for me.

I am a follower of Jesus, and that means I'm running after Him. Yes, I'm a leader in some ways, but I don't want to show up on some racetrack's leader board that merely shows I'm faster or more successful in my striving, that I'm ahead or behind others according to some worldly standard. I want to run the race the Lord has set before me, looking to my Savior, the author and perfecter of my faith (Hebrews 12:1–2). With fellow believers running beside me, "I press on toward the goal for the prize of the upward call of God in Christ Jesus" (Philippians 3:14). He has already called me; Christ has already made me His own (v. 12). With His strength and stamina, I press on!

We set our hope on God, who has the victory in Christ. Not our type of worldly personal victory but His victory for us. Not because our speed exceeds others' or because we check off more laps than anyone else but because we are—with our fellow believers—"more than conquerors through Him who loved us" (Romans 8:37). Running with me are my fellow Christian authors, for instance. I want their book sales and readership to be stellar! We may take turns carrying the baton or cheering each other on, but we are all in this vocation together; we have the same end goal of helping others learn and grow in their faith too.

Whatever your vocation, you can keep godly goals in front of you, cheer others on, and give God the glory in all you do.

JOURNAL

Write about times you've run in circles, hurrying . . . but realizing you were getting nowhere new. How does this devotion speak to you regarding the race of life you are running?

PRAYER

Father, forgive me for running this round-and-round race competitively. Help me keep my eyes on the prize, the One who has my victory sealed already . . .

CROWN OF LIFE

Blessed is the man who remains steadfast under trial, for when he has stood the test he will receive the crown of life, which God has promised to those who love Him. James 1:12

Did you ever dress up as a queen or princess, complete with a play crown or tiara? Maybe the crown was crafted to look like the real thing, with look-alike jewels and gold or silver paint. My play crown, placed upon my head, made me feel like I was powerful and important. But after lots of role-playing, the metallic finish faded, the fake jewels fell out, and my crown was eventually thrown away.

A real crown is a symbol of power and authority, worn by royalty. While many people in power are elected by citizens of a country, a king isn't elected; he is born into a family line to be king.

When Jesus was arrested and put on trial, Pilate asked if He was a king, and Jesus answered, "You say that I am a king. For this purpose I was born and for this purpose I have come into the world—to bear witness to the truth" (John 18:37). Jesus was born to be king, but His kingdom is not of this world. It is incomparably greater than any earthly kingdom, which will fade, fall apart, and end. He came to bear witness to the truth—to make a way for us to live with Him forever in His kingdom, and He did that when He died on the cross to save us from our sin. Three days later He rose, sealing His victory over sin, death, and the devil.

In this life, we will face trials and tribulations; Jesus said we would (John 16:33). Recorded in John's revelation to the churches are Jesus' words of forewarning that believers will suffer, face tribulation, and be tested by the devil. Jesus reassures His followers, exhorting them to remain steadfast:

Be faithful unto death, and I will give you the crown of life.
(Revelation 2:10)

We remain steadfast—faithful—in our tests and trials only because the One who called us is faithful; He is powerfully at work in us by the Spirit; He has overcome the world (John 16:33). May we share His purpose as we bear witness to the truth: Jesus Christ is Lord of lords and King of kings (Revelation 17:14)!

We are members of God's family, His children by faith in Christ.

> The Spirit Himself bears witness with our spirit that we are children of God, and if children, then heirs—heirs of God and fellow heirs with Christ. (Romans 8:16–17)

We won't receive the kind of crown that will fall apart, fade, or get thrown away. We'll receive a lasting crown, an "unfading crown of glory" (1 Peter 5:4) as heirs of His kingdom; the "crown of life, which God has promised to those who love Him."

Even now, Jesus is crowned in glory, seated at the right hand of the Father (Acts 2:33), and we will one day worship Him around His heavenly throne. On that day, we will receive immeasurably more than we can envision or imagine.

Amen. Come, Lord Jesus! (Revelation 22:20)

JOURNAL

Have you sported a crown? If so, share your story. What do you envision when you read "crown of life" or "unfading crown of glory"? Will it be golden and bejeweled, or do these phrases mean much more?

PRAYER

Heavenly Father, thank You for sending Your Son to be my Savior and King...

BRAND NEW

Behold, I am making all things new. Revelation 21:5

"It's bwoken, Gwandma! Can you fix it?!" With pieces of his toy in hand, my nephew ran to my loving mother-in-law, who wears an invisible super-woman cape in our family. A nurse by profession and a nurturer by heart, this woman has done more fixing—and helped with more healing—than many of us ever will. I watched as she sat at the table with a tube of super-glue and the broken pieces of his beloved toy. Patiently, she put each piece back together and held it in place until the glue was set. The toy was almost good as new.

Jesus takes our brokenness and makes us new. Even areas of my life that I may call healthy or whole are bent, marred, or chipped by sin's effects. Maybe they're in working condition, but barely. Yes, even the best parts of us are compromised. We can attempt to glue every shattered piece back together, but only Jesus can heal us. As we run to Him, we admit that we're broken. We can cry, "Fix it, Jesus!" and He already has.

By His wounds we are healed of our greatest brokenness: sin (Isaiah 53:5). From shattered shards to whole, we are fixed without seams or scars that would reveal our once-shattered state. He heals you and me com-pletely, no glue residue and no fault lines; He creates us new in Christ (2 Corinthians 5:17)! Even as we suffer or struggle in this life, God redeems our circumstances for *His purpose, our good, and His glory*.

His mercies never come to an end; they are new every morning (Lamentations 3:22–23). We receive daily renewal in Him. With the utmost care and patience, our Savior sits with us in our pain, puts the pieces back together as only He can, and holds us in place while we heal. In fact, He never leaves our side.

At the day of Christ, when He returns, our wholeness will be complete. Not just new but beyond imagination, better than new as we know it. In the apostle John's revelation to the churches, we read,

> Then I saw a new heaven and a new earth. . . . And I heard a loud voice from the throne saying, "Behold, the dwelling place of God is with man. He will dwell with them, and they will be His people, and God Himself will be with them as their God. He will wipe away every tear from their eyes, and death shall be no more, neither shall there be mourning, nor crying, nor pain anymore, for the former things have passed away." (Revelation 21:1, 3–4)

According to God's promise in Christ, He is making all things new (Revelation 21:5). So when we stare at shattered dreams, broken bodies, lost loved ones, or catastrophic events, we know for certain the promise that's already ours in Christ: new life—eternal life—in Him!

JOURNAL

Have you held broken pieces together with glue, stared at the seams, and wished you could make your mended item look brand new? Share how this analogy speaks to you and how it feels to know that you are made brand new in Christ.

PRAYER

Savior Jesus, with Your wounds I am healed. Thank You for Your mercies that are new every morning too . . .

FULLY PRESENT

This is the day that the LORD has made; let us rejoice
and be glad in it. Psalm 118:24

Seize the day. Capture the moment. Live life to the fullest. Every one of these common cliches makes me think of a favorite phrase of mine that is also along these lines: *Live fully present.* Think about that for a moment.

Oh sure, you and I know what it is to be present; to show up and do the thing, fulfill the commitment, or finish the job. But how often have we failed to fully invest in the moment because we instead pine for the past or preoccupy ourselves with concerns for the future?

I've been quick with a camera, eager to preserve vacation moments, birthday celebrations, and cross sections of family life. Too often I've failed to live fully present, because I was catching an angle or snapping a still shot and not simply basking in the moment or enjoying it. Understandably, I want to preserve that memory, but I'm not engaged in the moment or living fully present when I am distracted by that act of preservation.

Maybe we have captured a spectacular view through cellphone photos but failed to truly soak in the moment. We have attempted to seize control of something instead of seizing the day. We've lived more distracted than present. We come to Jesus for forgiveness, and we receive it, along with the Spirit's strength for today. True fullness of life is found in Him (John 10:10b), for this moment and for eternity. Because He lives in us, we can be fully present, valuing the people around us . . . or the view before us . . . or the moment that will soon pass.

In what moments would you like to be more mindful—to live fully present, by God's grace? Try these on for size:

- ♥ Step outside and take in God's creative work right in front of you. What does this particular piece of creation look like or how is it changing? Marvel at His handiwork that is familiar to you as you would a new view from another part of the world. God is actively at work in it. Shout out praise with the words of Psalm 118:24!

- Savor a milestone event as you're living it. Tune in to the conversations, relish the relationships embodied in the room, and honor the people around you with your full attention. "Outdo one another in showing honor" (Romans 12:10).

- Lose yourself in seemingly less significant moments too. What's unique about a particular moment? Are you alone with Jesus or sharing Him with someone else? What activity occupies your hands or your mind? Give yourself fully to it in that moment, thanking the Savior for it.

May we be hands-free (no camera required) so we can embrace a loved one in a hug or clap our hands with joy, fold our hands in prayer or lift them in praise.

By day the LORD commands His steadfast love, and at night His song is with me, a prayer to the God of my life. (Psalm 42:8)

JOURNAL

Choose one or more of the ideas for mindful moments described in today's devotion, and practice living fully present. Write about your experience.

PRAYER

God of my life, lead me by Your love to live fully present . . .

ABUNDANT LIFE

[Jesus said,] "I came that they may have life and
have it abundantly." John 10:10

I bundled up and joined my husband outside to shovel the heavy, wet snow. Our modern convenience (a snowblower) wouldn't start that morning, and we had limited time to get the snow cleared from the driveway and sidewalks. As we worked, I thought, *I'm cold. I'm wet. I'm weak, and this is really hard labor. Now, I'm tired. I'm sore. This is not my preferred form of exercise.* (You see, I do like to break a sweat, but on my terms.)

Most of the time, I am surrounded by so many modern conveniences and a level of relative comfort. That particular morning, I pondered: *Am I numb, indifferent, even resistant to discomfort?* Then I asked myself more probing questions: *How do I handle uncomfortable conversations, deal with emotional stress, or face spiritual battle? Do I seek distractions or substitutes instead of facing difficulties, enjoying richer relationships, or diving deeper into the Word? Gulp!* These were hard questions. Are they hard questions for you too?

My busy schedule provides an excuse to avoid tricky situations and deep conversations. I pursue food for comfort, coffee for energy, coffee for pleasure, coffee for reward (oh, dear, I see a pattern here). All joking aside . . . I also seek screentime for dopamine, especially when I'm looking for social media likes and affirmation. While some of these choices are not inherently bad, they provide less than I need. The same is true for you.

You and I want to live fully alive, don't we? And only the Lord can give us the abundant life (John 10:10b) we really need. He forgives us for the distractions we've created and the substitutes with which we've gorged ourselves. Out of *His inexhaustible love for us*, God does immeasurably more than all we could ask or imagine—more than any worldly substitute can offer—by the power of the Spirit working in you and in me.

Let's dive into His Word, where He comforts and strengthens us to face spiritual battles and other hard things ahead. Let's pursue His promises across Scripture, which all find their *yes* in Christ (2 Corinthians 1:20)! Let's follow the footsteps of the One who has given us abundant life in His name (John 20:31).

Oh, and by the way, it's okay to enjoy a cup of coffee along the way.

JOURNAL

Name your go-to distractions and substitutes. How do you avoid challenges? Where do you seek comfort or reward? As you consider each choice, contrast it with all that Jesus provides.

PRAYER

Dear God, forgive me for filling myself with substitutes and distractions when You offer immeasurably more. I want to live the abundant life, covered by Your grace in Christ . . .

EVERYTHING ABOUT YOU

In Him we live and move and have our being. Acts 17:28

You are God's masterpiece. A work of art. The pinnacle of His creation. You are His workmanship—and that means every working part of you, including the processes that operate seemingly autonomously. Yet He is the One who gives you every breath you take today. He knows the number of your days and the number of hairs on your head (Luke 12:7). Maybe, like me, you were created with only one wisdom tooth. (My family jokes about my lack of wisdom.) The Creator orchestrated each intricate detail and cares for it daily. Such intimate care is difficult for us to fathom, but it's true! King David said similarly of God's intimate care,

> Such knowledge is too wonderful for me; it is high; I cannot attain it. (Psalm 139:6)

The Lord walks with you, never leaving your side (Psalm 139:7–10). He knows your characteristics and your peculiarities. He knows your angst; He sees what makes your heart race and what causes your toes to curl. Maybe you have a taste for Asian cuisine . . . or exploration. Perhaps you prefer the comfort found in a good book or the adventure found on a hiking trail. He knows what fuels your passion; He designed you to delight in certain colors or distinct aromas, creative activities or active sports. (You may have an entirely different list of preferences. Did I get you thinking about your uniqueness?) The point is this: He knows everything about you.

> Your eyes saw my unformed substance; in Your book were written, every one of them, the days that were formed for me, when as yet there was none of them. (Psalm 139:16)

The Lord knew, before you were born, His plans for you, His purpose through you, His days formed for you. Our lives are not our own, and isn't that great news?

He Himself gives to all mankind life and breath and everything. . . . In Him we live and move and have our being. (Acts 17:25, 28)

Why would we try to claim anything different? To live as though we are self-made people? Why would we disregard the One who created us, redeemed us in Christ, and calls us His own? He alone knows the fullness of His purpose for us. *He alone provides all that we need* for life, both now and for eternity. Just as He knows everything about us, so He knows our repentant hearts too. The Lord forgives us for our faulty claims and every other sin. We have new life in Him, and that includes every breath that we take. With all of creation,

Let everything that has breath praise the LORD! (Psalm 150:6)

Praise the Lord!

JOURNAL

Have fun listing a number of your preferences, peculiarities, and characteristics, all a part of the unique creation that is YOU! Praise the Lord on this page for every part of you, including His plans and purpose prepared for you . . . and every breath you take!

PRAYER

Lord God, I praise You for Your intricate creation of me and Your intimate care of me . . .

TAKEN CAPTIVE

*Whatever is true, whatever is honorable, whatever is just, what-
ever is pure, whatever is lovely, whatever is commendable, if there
is any excellence, if there is anything worthy of praise, think
about these things.* Philippians 4:8

With a spring in my step, I hopped in my car and headed for home. My thoughts led the way: *Coffee time with my friend was so good today. I appreciate her friendship and the trust we have in one another. I hope I didn't over-share when I . . . Oh dear, I probably did. And then when she offered to help by . . . She probably thinks I'm beyond help. Oh, I bet she won't want to have coffee with me again. What if I just blew it by . . . ? Well, maybe that's for the best, since I don't deserve . . .*

Sometimes our thought patterns start and stay on point, driving us in a healthy direction. Other times, they wander all over the road, and soon we're steering toward a downward spiral and there's no stepping on the brakes. Take my meandering thoughts above, for instance. Before long, I was stuck in a deep ditch. Held captive.

I know that negative, worrisome, untrue, or gossipy thoughts want to invade my head space, and they do nothing to help fix a situation, remedy a relationship, or grow me into greater Christlikeness. So why do I allow them to take over the driver's seat?

My grandma used to tell me that thoughts give way → to words → to actions → to *life*. Will my life be one filled with integrity and a strong witness for my Savior? Or will my life goals be sidelined because my wandering mind has driven me to all kinds of unhealthy destinations? I want to steer my mind in healthier directions, but before I know it, I have swerved into unhealthy spaces, time and again.

2 Corinthians 10:5 exhorts us to "take every thought captive to obey Christ," but we often fail to obey. Forgive us, Lord! Christ was taken captive,

beaten, and crucified for our sins. Covered by His grace, we turn to His Word for transformation and the renewal of our minds (Romans 12:2). God the Spirit is active and working through the Word in miraculous ways to steer us back on track, pivoting our thoughts to "whatever is true, honorable, just, pure, lovely . . . worthy of praise."

The Lord can do immeasurably more in us than what we would attempt on our own, but it's not about striving in His Word either; it's about resting in it and living our lives according to it, by His grace. All the while, we recognize His presence, His power, and *His renewing work in our minds* . . . and in us.

With God guarding my heart and my mind (Philippians 4:7), I can "think about these things," pivot my spiraling thoughts, and replace them with a focus on true, excellent, and praiseworthy things. And I can put them into practice too (v. 9) ➔ for *life*.

JOURNAL

What thoughts attempt to take you captive? Are they typically negative or untrue, worrisome or gossipy? Share your thoughts regarding my grandma's words. Do you agree? Praise God for His protection and His strength to steer you back when you've wandered.

PRAYER

Lord God, continue Your transforming work in me, by the Holy Spirit. Guard my heart and mind in Christ . . .

LIGHT AND LIFE

Again Jesus spoke to them, saying, "I am the light of the
world. Whoever follows Me will not walk in darkness, but will
have the light of life." John 8:12

I can force a smile and fake it 'til I make it, but what others receive
from me will be disingenuous at best. I can slather sunless tanning lotion
on my face, but the artificial glow is limited, fleeting, and manufactured.
Incomparably greater is the genuine glow that shines forth from within me
as Jesus' light shines in my life where there was once darkness. You and I
are light in the Lord (Ephesians 5:8), filled with His brilliance, by faith.

Did you know that Moses' face literally shone after he had been with
the Lord? (See Exodus 34:29–35.) So great was the brilliance that he put a
veil over his face, in part because he didn't want the people to see the light
fade over time, the longer he'd been away from the Lord's direct presence
(2 Corinthians 3:7, 13). But we are continually light-bearers in Christ; we do
not depart from His presence; He is always with us. We don't have to veil
our faces for fear that others will witness a fading glow. "And we all, with
unveiled face, [behold] the glory of the Lord" (2 Corinthians 3:18). The light,
by His glorious grace, shines through us for the world to see.

I want to be that light-bearer, in continual fellowship with Jesus, but I
confess that sometimes I fall for lies told in darkness, and I start walking
that way. I am comforted by John's inspired words that first convict me,
then reveal the grace of God in Jesus, who leads me back to the light,
enabling my witness for Him in fellowship with others:

If we say we have fellowship with Him while we walk in darkness, we lie
and do not practice the truth. But if we walk in the light, as He is in the
light, we have fellowship with one another, and the blood of Jesus His
Son cleanses us from all sin. (1 John 1:6–7)

Sister in Christ, you shine from the inside out, not because you manufacture any light on your own, but because God has chosen you to be a vessel for His light in Christ. While we were once in darkness, He "has shone in our hearts to give the light of the knowledge of the glory of God in the face of Jesus Christ" (2 Corinthians 4:6). When someone says, "I see Jesus in you," that's because His light is shining through you!

We have eternal life in Jesus. And this life is the light of all people.

The light shines in the darkness, and the darkness has not overcome it. (John 1:5)

Imagine all that the light does in you—and will continue to do through you—as you *reflect Him to the world*. Your glow stokes the fire within fellow believers and leads them to let their light shine too.

You are the light of the world.... Let your light shine before others, so that they may see your good works and give glory to your Father who is in heaven. (Matthew 5:14, 16)

JOURNAL

Look up Psalm 34:5 and write it here. Describe what this verse means for you, as you live for Christ today.

PRAYER

God, "Be gracious to us and bless us and make [Your] face to shine upon us" (Psalm 67:1). Shine Your light through me, Jesus . . .

COME, LORD JESUS!

And I heard a loud voice from the throne saying, "Behold, the dwelling place of God is with man. He will dwell with them, and they will be His people, and God Himself will be with them as their God." Revelation 21:3

Another tragedy occurred in our community. Senseless acts of violence plague our nation. A child suffers at the hands of her abuser. Hard times hit another family. Every time we are overwhelmed by the evil and depravity in our world, evidence of sin's effects, we may cry out, "Come quickly, Lord Jesus!" I know I have. His return is certain, and it's getting closer, though no one knows the day. Jesus Himself said, "But concerning that day and hour no one knows, not even the angels of heaven, nor the Son, but the Father only" (Matthew 24:36).

May we be awake and waiting for Jesus' return, because that day will come like a thief in the night (1 Thessalonians 5:2). The Lord doesn't say this to scare us, but to reassure us, to remind us that His return is imminent, and to encourage us to be ready. We could not be prepared, apart from Christ's completed work on our behalf; He took our guilt and gave His life to save ours. *By faith, we have the Spirit* to strengthen, guide, and continue His work in us: "He who began a good work in you will bring it to completion at the day of Jesus Christ" (Philippians 1:6). He "will sustain you to the end, guiltless in the day of our Lord Jesus Christ" (1 Corinthians 1:8).

We were made for more than the life we're currently living. There's a longing in us because we were created for a life different than our present circumstances dictate and immeasurably better than this sin-filled world can offer us. Try as we might, we cannot be satisfied with lesser things.

Jesus is right now preparing a dwelling place for us . . . and He is coming back (John 14:3). Eternity will be, for all who believe, immeasurably more amazing than we can comprehend. He has set eternity in our hearts (Ecclesiastes 3:11), a hunger for heaven, a yearning for Jesus' return. May we long for eternal, heavenly things:

If then you have been raised with Christ, seek the things that are above, where Christ is, seated at the right hand of God. Set your minds on things that are above, not on things that are on earth. For you have died, and your life is hidden with Christ in God. When Christ who is your life appears, then you also will appear with Him in glory. (Colossians 3:1–4)

We can cry out, "Yes, Christ, You are my life!" With King David, we can confidently say, "I believe that I shall look upon the goodness of the Lord in the land of the living" (Psalm 27:13). Amen! In the final resurrection, we will look upon the goodness of the Lord—the Lord Himself! So we wait for Him, though we don't know the day.

Wait for the Lord; be strong, and let your heart take courage; wait for the Lord! (Psalm 27:14)

JOURNAL

What will help you keep your mind on "things that are above"? What do you find most reassuring or comforting about this final devotion? Choose one of the verses to write out and memorize as a regular reminder of Christ's imminent and glorious return.

PRAYER

Jesus Christ, You are my life! "Amen. Come, Lord Jesus!" (Revelation 22:20)

Notes

Notes _____

Notes _____

Notes

Notes

Notes _____